More
Practical Charts

20 additional chart types for data–savvy audiences
A companion book to Nick Desbarats' *Practical Charts*

Nicholas P. Desbarats

Practical Reporting, Inc.

Published by
Practical Reporting Inc.

P.O. Box 77021, RPO Old Ottawa South
Ottawa, ON K1S 5N2
Canada
www.practicalreporting.com
Email: info@practicalreporting.com

COPY EDITORS: Paulina Cossette and Bryan Pierce
COMPOSITION: Wayne Kehoe and Bryan Pierce
COVER DESIGN: Nick Desbarats
PRINTER AND BINDER: C&C Offset Printing Company

ISBN: 978-1-7388883-3-7

This book was printed on acid-free paper in China.

10 9 8 7 6 5 4 3 2 1

Table of Contents

Chapter 4: Showing how values are distributed across a range *(cont.)*

Chapter 5: Showing how variables are related   55

Chapter 5: Showing how variables are related *(cont.)*

What now?   85

Index   87

Introduction

What's in this book?
Who should read it?

> **IMPORTANT: This book is an optional companion to my *Practical Charts* book and isn't intended to be read on its own.** If you haven't read *Practical Charts* yet, go read that one first, then come back and read this one. It's OK; I'll wait.

WHAT'S IN THIS BOOK THAT ISN'T IN *PRACTICAL CHARTS*?

In *Practical Charts*, we saw about 30 "essential" chart types that...

- IMO, anyone who creates charts as part of their work should be aware of and understand when to use.
- Are, for the most part, familiar to audiences with "average" levels of data savviness, such as non-technical decision-makers.
- You might see in articles, presentations, books, etc., that are targeted at a general audience.

This book covers an additional 20 or so "advanced" chart types that...

- Might not be familiar to audiences with an average level of data savviness, who will likely require explanations to understand how to read them and who might struggle to understand those chart types, even with explanations.

- Might already be familiar to audiences with technical or scientific backgrounds.

- Generally aren't used in content that's intended for a general audience, but are used regularly in technical or scientific articles, presentations, reports, and the like .

The "advanced" chart types in this book are grouped into six categories (don't worry if you don't know what some of these are; we'll see plenty of examples in the book):

Pareto charts

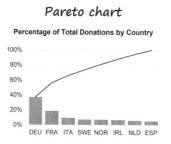

Pareto chart

Heatmaps and "shape size" charts

Heatmap

Shape size chart

Chart types for showing *cyclical (e.g., seasonal) time series data*

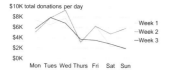

Overlapping cycles chart

Heatmap

Cycle plot

Chart types for showing how values are *distributed across a range*

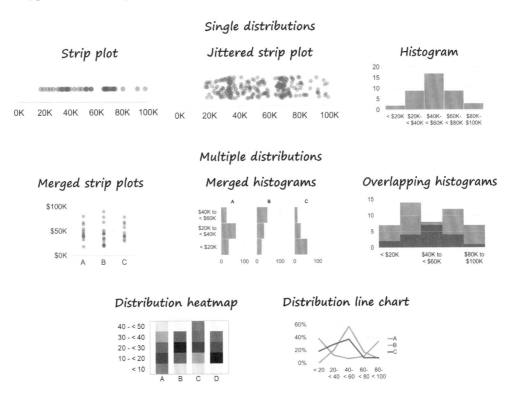

Chart types for showing how *variables are related*

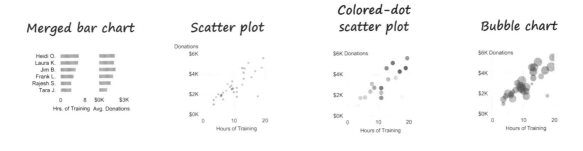

Chart types for showing *variable relationships changing over time*

I consider these to be very useful—but not essential—chart types for anyone who creates charts for audiences with above-average levels of data savviness in any industry, sector, or domain.

If you find yourself needing to use one of these advanced chart types but you're not sure if your audience has a high enough level of data savviness to understand it, you could use the "gentle reveal," "bait and switch," and "duh insights" tricks that we saw in *Practical Charts* to explain the new chart type to them. If, however, you're worried that your audience might not have a high enough level of data savviness (or patience) to grasp one of these advanced chart types—even with explanations—I'd avoid using it. There's no point in showing a chart that the audience won't understand. In those situations, you might instead be able to communicate insights using more familiar (but less informative) chart types, bullet points on a slide, or text in a report.

> If these advanced chart types aren't "essential," why use them? Why not just stick to the basic ones that most audiences know how to read?

Yes, as a general rule, I recommend favoring simple, familiar chart types like bar charts and line charts because those chart types almost always require less cognitive effort to read for audiences with *any* level of data savviness. As we'll see throughout this book, though, advanced chart types allow you to communicate entire classes of valuable insights that would be difficult or impossible to convey using simpler, more familiar chart types, so there are times when there are real benefits to using them.

Another major reason to use advanced chart types is that they can be very useful when *analyzing data on your own* to discover useful patterns and relationships in data. While simple chart types like bar charts and line charts can be extremely useful for data analysis, there are certain types of insights that are much more obvious in more advanced chart types, or that simply *can't* be spotted using basic chart types. If you discover a useful insight using an advanced chart type that your audience might not understand, you can often communicate that insight to them using simpler chart types or bullet points.

A *bad* reason to use advanced chart types is to show off. Using an advanced chart type simply to demonstrate your knowledge of advanced chart types puts your own interests above those of your audience, which I don't recommend. If a simpler, more familiar chart type will do the trick in a given situation, use it. It will minimize the cognitive effort that the audience needs to spend on reading it, regardless of their level of data savviness.

> How "advanced" are we talking, here?

Well, "advanced" is a relative term. If you have a background in statistics or mathematics, you probably won't find the chart types in this book to be particularly "advanced" because most of them are taught in secondary school or in undergraduate courses. Indeed, you might be familiar with even more advanced chart types that aren't covered in this book. If you do have a stats or math background, though, you'll probably still learn important skills from this book regarding how to better design these chart types to effectively communicate insights to audiences with any level of data savviness.

If, however, math class is a foggy memory of things that you forgot immediately after the exam and never used again, some of these chart types might feel "advanced" to you. I suspect that you'll be able to grasp them pretty easily with my brilliant explanations, though 🙂, which you can ~~steal~~ use as inspiration to explain these chart types and techniques to your audiences, if necessary.

> Why did you separate these advanced chart types into a second book? Why not just include them in *Practical Charts*?

Many chart creators will only ever create charts for audiences with average levels of data savviness and will, therefore, never be able to use the advanced chart types in this book. I didn't want to force those chart creators to buy and read content that they'll never use, so I decided to put it in a separate book for those who will be able to use it.

Alright, enough with the boring intro stuff. Let's see some actual chart types!

In *Practical Charts*, we saw five chart types for showing the breakdown of a single total:

In this book, I want to add one more that's a little harder to grasp but that can be very useful in certain situations, called…

Chapter 1

Pareto charts

BEFORE I EXPLAIN what a Pareto chart is, a quick reminder that, as we saw in *Practical Charts*, stacked bar charts are useful for showing *cumulative subtotals* of parts within a total:.

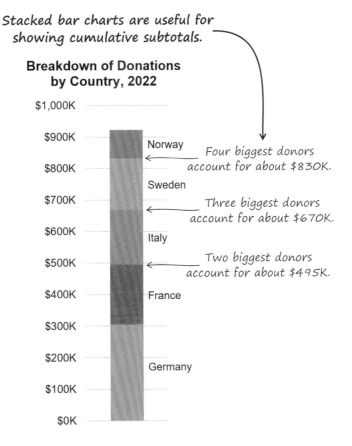

Stacked bar charts are useful for showing cumulative subtotals.

Breakdown of Donations by Country, 2022

Four biggest donors account for about $830K.

Three biggest donors account for about $670K.

Two biggest donors account for about $495K.

As we also saw, stacked bar charts generally turn into busy-looking spaghetti charts if there are more than six or seven parts. What if you had donation values for, say, 15 countries instead of the 5 that are in the stacked bar chart above, but you still needed to show cumulative subtotals of parts? In a situation like that, you could switch from a stacked bar chart to a *Pareto chart*:

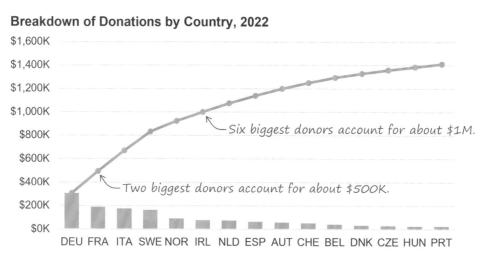

A "Pareto chart"

Breakdown of Donations by Country, 2022

In this Pareto chart, the donations for each country are shown as bars along the bottom, and the line is a cumulative subtotal of the countries (see blue callouts above for clarification). Like stacked bar charts, Pareto charts allow subtotals of parts to be seen easily, but, unlike stacked bar charts, Pareto charts can show more than 6 or 7 values—up to 25 or so—without looking overly busy.

Like any chart type, Pareto charts have weaknesses, as well:

- In a Pareto chart, **the "parts" bars inevitably end up getting "crushed"** down near the zero line because they're always much smaller than the "cumulative total" values (the points in the line), and the total and parts are shown on the same quantitative scale. This can make it tough to make precise comparisons among the parts.

- Compared with a stacked bar chart or pie chart, a Pareto chart **doesn't make it as visually obvious what fraction of the total each part represents.** Just as in a regular bar chart, the audience must estimate the values of the bars based on the textual quantitative scale, and then convert those textual values into mental representations of fractions of a total. Stacked bar charts and pie charts skip most of those cognitive steps.

- I've seen **many audiences get confused by the line in a Pareto chart.** As we saw in *Practical Charts*, many audiences automatically assume "time" when they see a line chart, but the scale in a Pareto usually *isn't* time.

- Pareto charts aren't a common chart type, so **there's a good chance that the audience won't have seen one before.** You may need to use the "gentle reveal," "bait and switch," and/or "duh insights" tricks if you need to show one to your audience.

Stacked bar charts are better than Pareto charts in all of these respects, so I'd only use a Pareto chart if there were too many parts to fit comfortably in a stacked bar chart.

Some of the downsides of Pareto charts can be overcome by using an alternative Pareto chart design that I've been using for the past few years and that, in my experience, audiences seem to grasp more easily than the traditional Pareto chart design that we just saw:

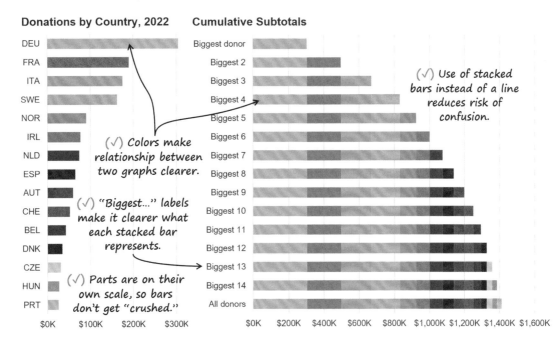

A potentially friendlier Pareto chart design

I've found that audiences find this alternative design easier to understand than the traditional Pareto chart design, but you can, of course, decide which one to use with your audiences.

Both the traditional and alternative Pareto chart designs generally work well when they include up to about 25 parts but can start to look overcrowded beyond that. What if your data contains more than 25 parts, though? At that point, the best option is probably a treemap, like those we saw in *Practical Charts*. Although cumulative subtotals can't be perceived as easily in a treemap as they can in a Pareto chart, you could, for example, make a group of parts of a treemap a different color and compare that group of parts to the total. It's not great, but it's the best option that I'm aware of in that kind of situation.

> ### Key takeaways: Pareto charts
>
> - When showing the breakdown of a total that consists of roughly 7 to 25 parts and you need to feature subtotals of parts, consider using a Pareto chart.
> - If there are few enough parts to fit comfortably in a stacked bar chart, consider using a stacked bar chart instead of a Pareto chart.
> - If there are more than roughly 25 parts, consider using a treemap.

Now that you know what Pareto charts are and when to use them, we can update the "Breakdown of a total" decision tree from *Practical Charts* to include them:

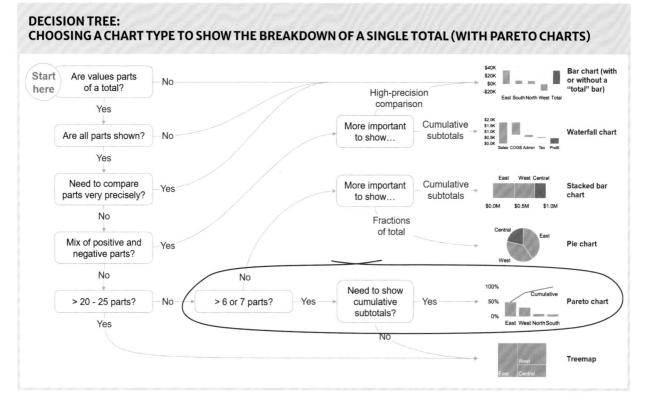

DECISION TREE:
CHOOSING A CHART TYPE TO SHOW THE BREAKDOWN OF A SINGLE TOTAL (WITH PARETO CHARTS)

Let's move on to the next group of advanced charts that are important to know about, which are…

Chapter 2

Heatmaps and shape size charts

I'LL EXPLAIN WHAT a "shape size chart" is in a moment, but for now, let's start with one that you're probably already familiar with:

HEATMAPS

In *Practical Charts*, we saw that it's usually a good idea to use a sequential color palette to identify sequential categories:

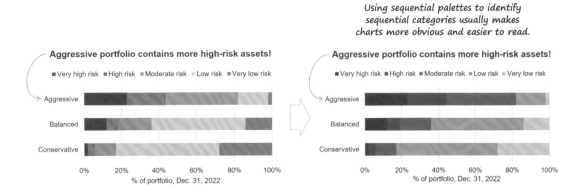

Using sequential palettes to identify sequential categories usually makes charts more obvious and easier to read.

There's another common use of sequential palettes, which is to show different *quantities* as lighter or darker color shades, which produces a "heatmap."

We already saw several heatmaps in *Practical Charts*:

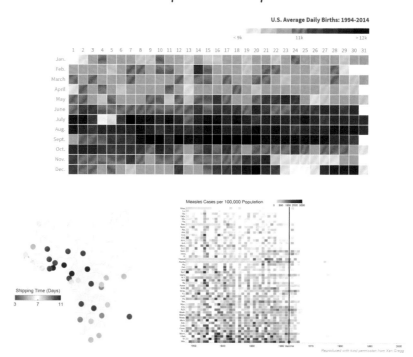

Examples of "heatmaps"

Even though these are all different chart types (time series, map, etc.), they all represent quantities as lighter and darker color shades, which means they're *also* heatmaps.

You probably agreed that it made sense to use a heatmap in these situations, but it's worth asking: *Why?* What is it about these scenarios that makes a heatmap a better choice than, say, a bar chart or line chart?

What these scenarios all have in common is that patterns, outliers, or other types of insights needed to be shown among a *large number of values*. The birthday heatmap above, for example, is designed to show patterns among 366 values (365 "regular" days plus the February 29th "Leap Day"). The designer of that chart could have shown 366 bars of different lengths instead of a heatmap of 366 colored squares, but, as you can imagine, a 366-bar chart would be very visually busy and would make it considerably harder to spot patterns than in the heatmap version.

Similarly, for the "measles cases" heatmap above, the chart creator could have shown a stack of 51 individual lines instead of 51 rows of colored squares, but 51 lines would be very visually busy and would make it harder to spot patterns of interest than in the heatmap version.

That's the main advantage of heatmaps: **When showing a large number of values, heatmaps are less visually overwhelming and make patterns, outliers, etc., more obvious than they would be as bars, lines, or other chart types.** For example, the heatmap below shows sales revenue for 24 stores across 17 product categories (so, 408 values). Despite showing hundreds of values, it's not visually overwhelming, and many potentially useful patterns and outliers are immediately noticeable:

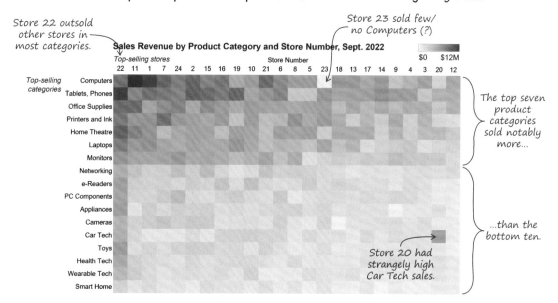

Heatmaps make patterns, exceptions, etc., obvious when showing many values.

If these same values were shown as a non-heatmap chart, such as a bar chart, it would look busier, and the patterns and outliers would be less obvious:

(!) Bar charts, line charts, and other "non-heatmap" charts are visually busier, and patterns, exceptions, etc., aren't as obvious when showing many values.

Sales Revenue by Product Category and Store Number, Sep. 2022

Top-selling stores / Store Number / $0 $12M

Top-selling categories	22	11	1	7	24	2	15	16	19	10	21	6	8	5	23	18	13	17	14	9	4	3	20	12
Computers																								
Tablets, Phones																								
Office Supplies																								
Printers and Ink																								
Home Theatre																								
Laptops																								
Monitors																								
Networking																								
e-Readers																								
PC Components																								
Appliances																								
Cameras																								
Car Tech																								
Toys																								
Health Tech																								
Wearable Tech																								
Smart Home																								

If heatmaps are more effective in these situations, why not use heatmaps for *all* charts, even those that show a *small* number of values?

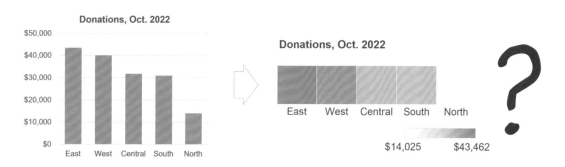

Like every chart type, heatmaps have their weaknesses, the main one being that they only allow the audience to perceive the values in a chart with *low precision*. You can see this in the bar chart and heatmap above: Although it's very easy to estimate the values in the bar chart on the left to within a few percentage points of their true values, it's harder to estimate the values in the heatmap version on the right, and your estimates probably won't be nearly as accurate. Sure, you can spot high and low values immediately in the heatmap, but it's hard to tell *precisely* what those values are or to make precise comparisons (try to estimate, for example, how much greater the West is than the Central region).

Therefore, **when showing a small number of values, it's generally better to use bar charts, line charts, and other non-heatmap chart types.** When showing a small number of values, those chart types aren't visually overwhelming and they allow the audience to spot patterns, outliers, and other insights more easily, precisely, and reliably than heatmaps do.

You might see charts in the wild that show a small number of values as a heatmap, but there are usually better, non-heatmap alternatives. For example, the chart below on the left shows sales as bar length, and profit margin percentage as heatmap colors:

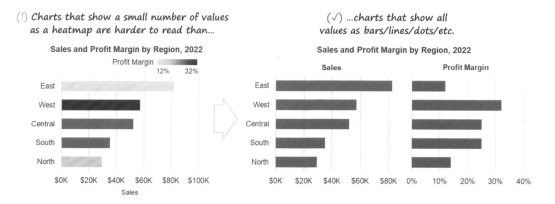

A non-heatmap chart of the same values (e.g., the merged bar chart above on the right) allows the audience to see and compare profit margin values more easily and precisely than when those values are shown as heatmap colors, and it isn't visually overwhelming because only a small number of values are being shown.

> **Key takeaways: Heatmaps**
>
> • Consider using a heatmap when you need to show patterns, outliers, etc., among a large number of values.
> • Avoid using a heatmap to show a small number of values. Consider a bar chart, line chart, or other higher-precision chart type instead.

In addition to heatmaps, there's another chart type that's often a good option when you need to show patterns and outliers among a large number of values, namely…

"SHAPE SIZE" CHARTS

In situations when it makes sense to use a heatmap, showing values as *smaller or larger shapes* is usually also a viable option. We saw a few examples of charts that show values as shape size in *Practical Charts*, and we'll see a few more in later chapters of this book:

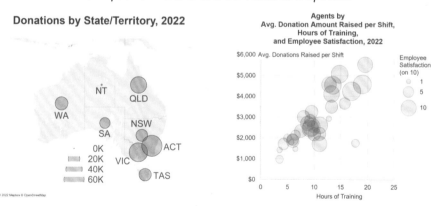

Examples of charts that show values as shape size.

Charts that represent quantities as shapes of different sizes are sometimes called "proportional symbol charts," but I prefer the friendlier term "shape size charts." Like heatmaps, **shape size charts are good at showing patterns, outliers, etc., among a large number of values without becoming visually overwhelming.** Also, like heatmaps, they only allow the audience to estimate and compare values with low precision, since it's hard to precisely compare the sizes of shapes.

When should you go with a shape size chart rather than a heatmap? The bad news is that a variety of factors need to be considered to determine whether a heatmap or a shape size chart will be a more effective choice in a given situation (see table below). The good news is that, if you try visualizing your data as both a heatmap and a shape size chart and then compare the two versions, one of them will usually stand out as the obviously better choice for the situation at hand. In the rare cases when one isn't obviously better than the other, either choice will probably work well.

What, exactly, are the factors that affect whether to choose a heatmap or a shape size chart in a given situation?

Heatmaps *are generally a more effective choice when one or more of the following are true…*	Shape size charts *are generally a more effective choice when one or more of the following are true…*
• Values are arranged in a grid or other *regular* arrangement (in a table, in a circle, etc.).	• Values *aren't* arranged in a grid or other regular arrangement (i.e., on a map, in a scatter plot, etc.).
• Very small values are important.	• Very small values are unimportant (in a shape size chart, they might be so small as to be almost unnoticeable).
• Making proportional comparisons ("this value is twice as much as that value," etc.) is relatively *un*important.	• Making proportional comparisons is relatively important (quantities can be compared a little more precisely based on shape size than based on different color shades).
• All values fall within a narrow range that's far from zero, and it's important to feature the small differences among them.	• The values don't fall within a narrow range that's far from zero, or they do fall within a narrow range but the small differences among them don't need to be featured.
• It's certain that the chart will be viewed in color (on a color monitor, printed on a color printer, etc.).	• It's possible that the chart will be viewed in black and white (printed on a black and white printer, photocopier, fax machine, etc.).

If you need to show a large number of values for *two* variables, you could combine shape sizes and heatmap colors. The resulting charts can be pretty cool but may be too complex for some audiences:

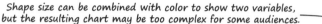

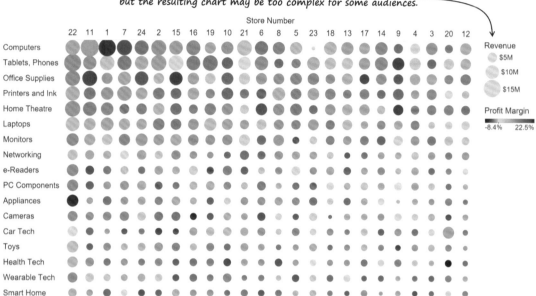

Shape size can be combined with color to show two variables, but the resulting chart may be too complex for some audiences.

Key takeaways: Shape size charts

- Consider using a shape size chart or a heatmap when you need to show patterns, outliers, etc., among a large number of values.
- Try visualizing the data as both a shape size chart and a heatmap to determine which is the best option for the situation at hand.
- Avoid using a shape size chart to show a small number of values. Consider a bar chart, line chart, or other higher-precision chart type instead.

Formatting shape size charts

If you decide to go with a shape size chart, there are a few formatting guidelines to keep in mind:

- Shapes other than circles (squares, hexagons, etc.) can be used in shape size charts, but the more complex the shape, the harder it will be to compare the sizes of those shapes, and the more visually busy the chart will get. Circles are the simplest shape, so circular "bubbles" are usually the best choice.

- In a shape size chart where the shapes aren't arranged in a grid, circle, or other regular pattern (e.g., shapes on a map, shapes in a bubble chart, etc.), it's important to make the shapes semitransparent with a thin border so that, if one shape ends up overlapping another, the shape that's underneath will still be visible.

- When designing a shape size chart, you'll need to choose a *scale* for the shapes (i.e., how generally large or small to make them). There's no hard-and-fast rule for choosing a scale for shapes, but, as a rule of thumb, try to make the shapes as large as possible until shapes start to overlap one another significantly or start to look ridiculously big.

Hopefully, you now feel comfortable deciding when it does and doesn't make sense to use heatmaps and shape size charts, so let's move on to the next important group of "advanced" chart types, which are chart types for…

Chapter 3

Showing cyclical (e.g., seasonal) time series data

SOME TIME SERIES data has *cycles*; for example, the daily donation data in the chart below seems to have some kind of repeating pattern:

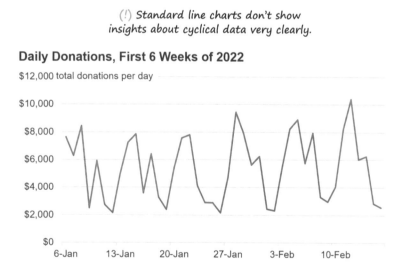

(!) Standard line charts don't show insights about cyclical data very clearly.

Daily Donations, First 6 Weeks of 2022

There's clearly a repeating cycle in this data, but that's just about the only thing that's clear when looking at it as a standard line chart. It looks like the cycle is probably weekly, but even that's hard to say for sure. If it *is* weekly, which days of the week tend to be higher or lower? How do the six weeks in this chart compare with one another? How did the weekly pattern change during those six weeks? Hmm…

A simple improvement would be to mark off the cycle periods by, for example, shading the weekends:

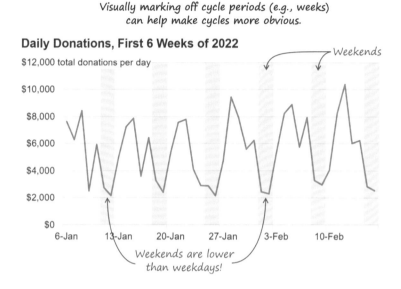

OK, it's now clear that each cycle is indeed one week long and that donations dip on weekends. But it's still hard or impossible to answer most of the other questions that I mentioned, so if those are the types of insights that you need to communicate, you'll need a few new chart types that we haven't seen yet, such as…

OVERLAPPING CYCLES CHARTS

If you need to show how cycles compare with one another, you could use an "overlapping cycles" chart. The overlapping cycles chart below shows six weeks of daily donation data, but the six weeks are now "overlapped" to make them easier to compare:

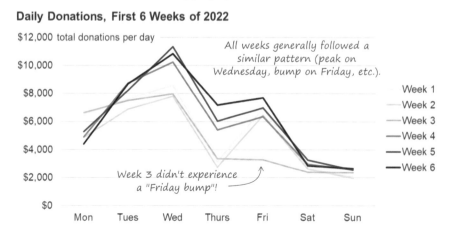

This isn't really a distinct chart type *per se*, it's just a standard line chart with the data arranged in a particular way. It's a very useful technique that often doesn't occur to chart creators, though, so I've included it in this book. This "overlapping cycles" technique can also work with other types of line charts that we saw in *Practical Charts*, such as step charts.

What if you needed to compare, say, 15 weeks instead of 6? As you can imagine, an overlapping cycles chart with 15 lines would be visually overwhelming. What's the go-to move that we saw in the previous chapter for showing a large number of values without the chart becoming visually overwhelming? That's right, we could switch to…

HEATMAPS (FOR SHOWING CYCLICAL TIME SERIES)

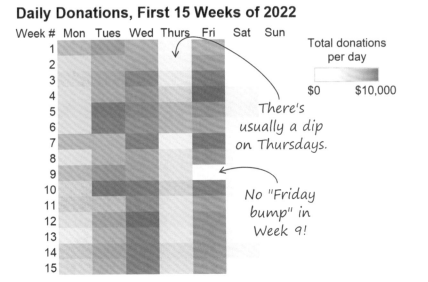

This heatmap shows many values (15 weeks × 7 days per week) but is less visually overwhelming than a 15-line overlapping cycles chart. As we saw in the last chapter, the superpower of heatmaps is that they allow you to show patterns and outliers among many values without becoming visually overwhelming, and this is a good example of that superpower in action. As we also saw, though, the tradeoff (there's always a tradeoff…) is that you lose some precision; for example, in the heatmap above, it's hard to tell what the *precise* donation amount was on any given day. You can still show lots of interesting insights, though, such as the ones in the blue callouts above.

What if you needed to say something about how the *individual periods* within each cycle (e.g., the days of the week) changed over time—for example, whether Mondays got better or worse during a six-week period? To show those types of insights, you can use a lesser-known—but very useful—chart type called…

CYCLE PLOTS

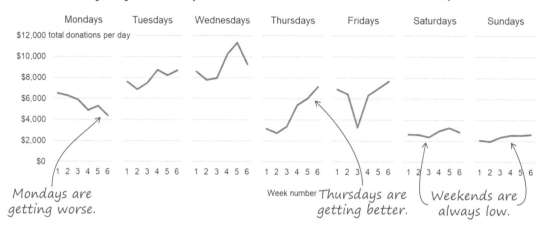

A "cycle plot"

Donations by Day of Week | Six weeks from Jan. 6-13 to Feb. 9-16, 2022

Mondays are getting worse.

Thursdays are getting better.

Weekends are always low.

Week number

Technically, cycle plots are just standard line charts that are arranged in a particular way, but because it's such a clever way, they have their own name. Note that some dataviz products allow cycle plots to be created with just a few clicks, but others require some manual copying and pasting of data and charts. As I mentioned in *Practical Charts*, Google is your friend (well, not really) if you're not sure how to create a cycle plot or any other chart type in your dataviz software product.

In all the chart examples in this chapter, the cycles were weekly cycles of days, but these same chart types and techniques work for cycles of other periods of time (monthly cycles of days, annual cycles of months, daily cycles of hours, etc.).

Now that you know about these additional chart types for showing data over time and when to use them, we can update the "showing data over time" decision tree in *Practical Charts* to include them:

DECISION TREE:
CHOOSING A CHART TYPE TO SHOW DATA OVER TIME (WITH CYCLICAL TIME CHARTS ADDED)

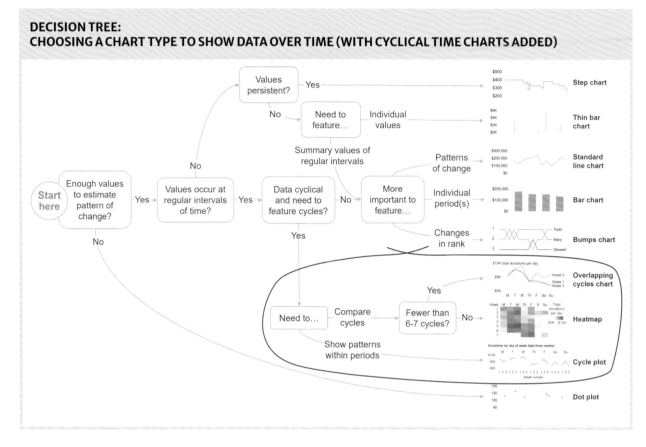

On to the next family of "advanced" chart types, which are for…

Chapter 4

Showing how values are distributed across a range

SAY YOU HAVE a table of employee salaries:

Employee Salaries

George L	$17,155	Maria D.	$40,051	Heshel S.	$64,285
Carlos O.	$19,551	Adriana N.	$41,695	Desideria C.	$66,782
Rumena A.	$26,885	Jessica H.	$44,653	Keith W.	$67,882
Safiye N.	$22,235	Kim L.	$46,565	Gaiana S.	$67,998
Laura D.	$22,562	Nora T.	$47,465	Sarah B.	$68,552
James K.	$24,562	Richard J.	$48,707	Brendan M.	$69,324
Otto L.	$30,426	Coby D.	$49,853	Jordaan P.	$70,415
Elea A.	$32,142	Malcolm S.	$50,148	Kyouko A.	$73,898
Anastasios T.	$33,482	Hermanni S.	$52,045	Rupert B.	$74,562
Curtis J.	$34,256	Shou J.	$56,990	Liana B.	$80,500
Pavao K.	$35,462	Valentina C.	$59,987	Ralf L.	$84,882
Connor J.	$36,782	Jyoti M.	$60,788	Maximiano P.	$97,852
Chipo R.	$37,562	Rudolf I.	$61,113		
Kayleah P.	$37,885	Aroldo F.	$61,921		

You can get *some* insights about this data when it's shown in a table like this. For example, because the table is sorted, you can easily see that the range of salaries is about $17K to $98K. Beyond that, though, it would require a fair amount of cognitive effort to see how these salaries are *distributed* across that range. For example, it's not immediately clear whether…

- There are any *clusters* (small salary ranges with many employees in them)

- There are any *gaps* (salary ranges with no employees in them)

- There are any *outliers* (values that are much smaller or much bigger than most of the others)

Showing this data in a bar chart makes it a bit easier to see these kinds of "distribution-related" insights:

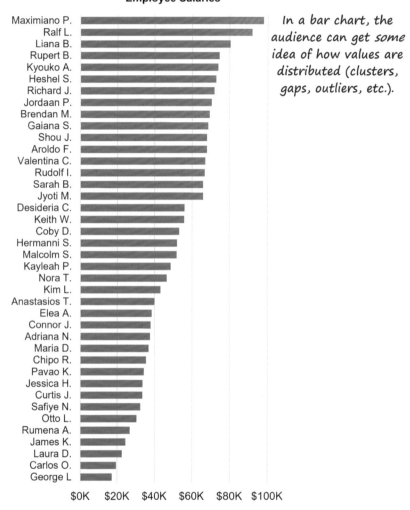

Employee Salaries

In a bar chart, the audience can get some idea of how values are distributed (clusters, gaps, outliers, etc.).

This is definitely more informative than a table of numbers, since patterns like the two outliers at the top and the lack of employees around $60K are more obvious. Is there a way to make those distribution-related insights even more obvious? Yes, in fact, there are several chart types that are specifically designed for…

SHOWING HOW A SINGLE SET OF VALUES IS DISTRIBUTED

Such as...

Strip plots

A strip plot shows values as dots along a quantitative scale, so a strip plot of the employee salary data that we were just looking at would look like this:

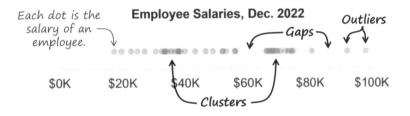

Ah! In this strip plot, distribution-related patterns such as clusters, gaps, outliers, etc., are even more obvious than in the bar chart.

Note that the dots in the strip plot above are semitransparent. This is because there could be identical values in the data (e.g., several employees with the same salary), and, if the dots were a solid color, those identical values would look like one, single dot/employee, and the audience wouldn't see that there are several identical values in the data, which could be important. If the dots are semitransparent, however, several dots in the same place will look darker, telling the audience that there are multiple identical values at that point on the strip plot.

> **Key takeaways: Strip plots**
>
> - To show how a set of values is distributed across a range, consider using a strip plot.
> - Consider making the dots in a strip plot semitransparent.

Let's take a big step back and ask if it's even necessary to show data like this as a graph in the first place? After all, if you just wanted to give the audience a general sense of what the salaries are in this company, why not just show them the average (or, more technically, the "arithmetic mean") salary for the company, which, in this case, works out to about $52K?

Well, let's say you're showing salaries for four companies instead of just one, and all those companies (coincidentally) have an average salary of $52K:

All these companies have an average salary of $52K!

Company A

$0K $20K $40K $60K $80K $100K

Company B

$0K $20K $40K $60K $80K $100K

Company C

$0K $20K $40K $60K $80K $100K

Company D

$0K $20K $40K $60K $80K $100K

If you only showed the average salaries of these four companies without showing any graphs, the audience would assume that these companies are all very similar in terms of salaries. The strip plots show that that's not true at all, however! Company B, for example, is a very different company than Company D when it comes to salaries, but that crucial information is hidden if only averages are shown. Unfortunately, many chart creators show averages without also showing distribution graphs alongside those averages, which can lead to very wrong insights and conclusions about the data.

> **Key takeaway: Showing distribution graphs alongside averages**
>
> - Avoid only showing averages without also showing distribution graphs, such as strip plots, along with the averages.

Now that I've (hopefully) sold you on how important it is to show distribution graphs, let's look at a few more useful distribution chart types.

In the scenario that we just saw, there were 40 employees. What if there were more, though? Say, 240? A strip plot might start to look like a solid line of overlapping dots, which isn't very meaningful:

(!) Strip plots can turn into meaningless lines of overlapping dots when there are many values.

Employee Salaries, Dec. 2022

$0K $20K $40K $60K $80K $100K

In that case, you could switch to...

Jittered strip plots

If your strip plot looks like a solid line of overlapping dots, you could switch to a *jittered strip plot*, which "spreads the dots out" to make clusters, gaps, etc., easier to see when there are many values:

A "jittered strip plot" can show more values.

Employee Salaries, Dec. 2022

Note that, in the jittered strip plot above, the vertical position of each dot is randomly generated for the sole purpose of "spreading the dots out" and doesn't represent anything. Also note that the width of the area over which the dots are spread should be just wide enough to show individual dots without excessive overlap, but not wider, since that could distort the audience's perception of the data or make the jittered strip plot look like a *scatter plot* (which we'll see later in the book), which it definitely isn't.

Let's keep pushing. Let's say that, instead of hundreds of employees, you had thousands. A jittered strip plot could turn into a solid block of overlapping dots in that case, which, again, wouldn't be very meaningful:

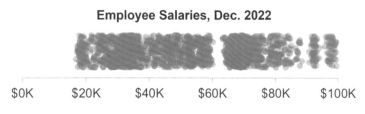

(!) Jittered strip plots can also become meaningless blocks of overlapping dots when there are many values.

Employee Salaries, Dec. 2022

In that case, you could switch to…

Histograms

Histo-whats?

You probably learned about histograms in secondary school, but, on the off chance that that knowledge is a bit foggy for you at this point in your life, let's have a refresher:

To make the histogram below, I divided the entire range of employee salaries into five intervals ($0K to < $20K, $20K to < $40K, etc.) that, in the context of histograms, are usually called "bins" for some strange reason. I then showed the number of employees in each bin as a bar chart, which produced the histogram below:

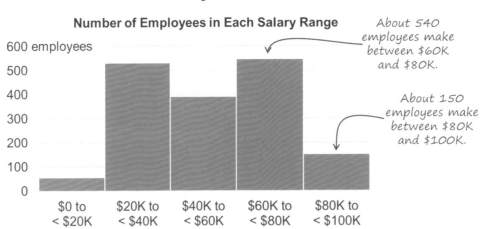

A "histogram"

Number of Employees in Each Salary Range

About 540 employees make between $60K and $80K.

About 150 employees make between $80K and $100K.

You might have noticed that the gaps between the bars in this histogram are very narrow. Traditionally, histograms are designed this way for reasons that aren't worth going into, but this convention is a useful "visual clue" for audiences who are familiar with histograms since it immediately tells them that they're looking at a histogram and not a "regular" bar chart, so I follow that convention.

Compared with strip plots and jittered strip plots, histograms have several important advantages:

1. Histograms **can show any number of values** (millions of values, billions of values, etc.) without looking crowded.

2. Histograms **make the overall "shape" of a distribution** (bell-shaped, U-shaped, flat, irregular, etc.) **clearer than strip plots.**

3. If the insight to be communicated involves comparing the number of values in different bins (e.g., comparing the number of employees who make $20K to < $40K to the number of employees who make $40K to < $60K), **histograms make such comparisons much easier than strip plots.** Those types of comparisons aren't needed very often in practice, however.

If histograms have all those advantages over strip plots, why not just use histograms to show distributions instead of strip plots all the time?

As with any other chart type, histograms have their weaknesses:

1. To many audiences, histograms are **harder to understand** than strip plots and are more "abstract."

2. Histograms are **less precise** than strip plots because they don't show individual values. For example, the histogram above doesn't show how much the lowest-paid employee makes, only that it's somewhere between $0 and $20K.

3. Histograms generally **aren't very meaningful when showing small numbers of values,** but strip plots can be.

If you find yourself needing to use a histogram but are unsure whether your audience knows how to read one, you can include some "duh insights," such as the two blue callouts in the histogram above, to help the audience quickly figure out how to read it.

Note that, when you create a histogram, you need to decide how many bins it will have, and the bars in the histogram will change based on how many bins you choose. In the histogram of salaries that we just saw, for example, if I'd chosen to show ten bins of $10K instead of five bins of $20K, the bars would have looked different. This begs the obvious question: How many bins should you choose for a histogram?

Unfortunately, there's no hard-and-fast rule for choosing the number of bins for a histogram. As with so many other design decisions, it depends on the specific job that the chart was created to do. For example, three insights that you might want to communicate about the same set of employee salaries are shown below. As you can see, each insight is best illustrated by a different number of bins:

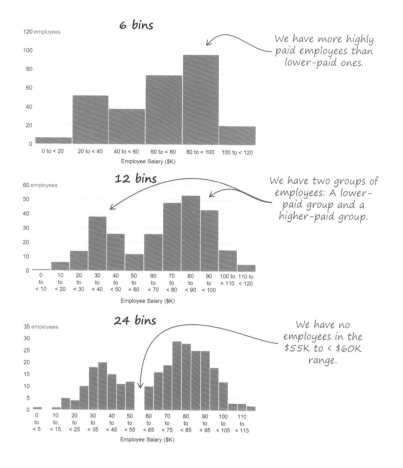

Is any one of these the "optimal" number of bins? Nope. The "optimal" number of bins depends on what, specifically, you need to say about the data.

If you Google "how to choose number of bins for histogram," however, you'll find a variety of methods for "calculating the optimal number of bins" based on the data to be visualized. Those calculations always recommend the same number of bins for a given data set regardless of the specific insight or answer that the chart is designed to communicate in the first place, though. I don't think you can "calculate the optimal number of bins" without taking the specific job of the chart into account, so, IMHO, any calculations that you might come across won't be reliable.

So, how do I suggest that you choose the number of bins for a histogram in practice? The best guidance I can offer is: "Choose the number of bins that best illustrates the specific insight that you need to communicate about the data." This usually means trying several different bin counts to find the one that best illustrates what you need to say about the data. For more details on choosing bin counts for histograms, visit practicalreporting.com/pc-resources, and click "How many bins should my histogram have?"

Key takeaways: Histograms

- Consider using a histogram, rather than a strip plot, to show how values are distributed across the range of a data set if: 1) there are many values in the data set, 2) showing the shape of the distribution is more important than showing individual values, or 3) the insight to be communicated requires comparing value counts of bins.
- When creating a histogram, choose the number of bins that best communicates the insight or answer that the chart is intended to communicate.

As usual, let's recap what we've learned about these chart types in a simple...

DECISION TREE:
CHOOSING A CHART TYPE TO SHOW HOW A SINGLE SET OF VALUES IS DISTRIBUTED

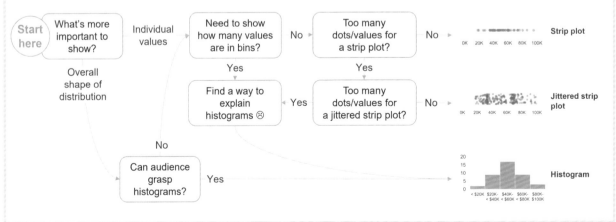

Now that we have some good options for showing how a single set of values is distributed across a range, we should talk about…

COMPARING HOW *MULTIPLE* SETS OF VALUES ARE DISTRIBUTED

Hopefully, you now have an appreciation for how useful it can be to show how a *single* set of values is distributed, so we can now take the next step and look at comparing how *multiple* sets of values are distributed. We got a taste of how informative this can be in the previous section when we compared the distributions of employee salaries of four companies (i.e., four sets of values) using strip plots:

There are other chart types that we haven't seen yet and that are useful for comparing the distributions of multiple sets of values in different situations:

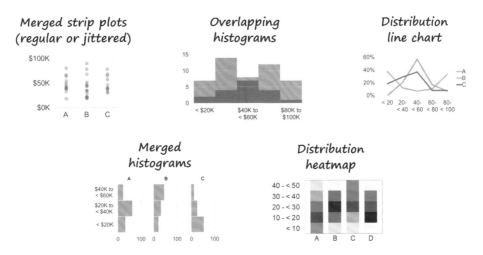

Let's start with the chart type that I use most often in practice to compare the distributions of multiple sets of values:

Merged strip plots

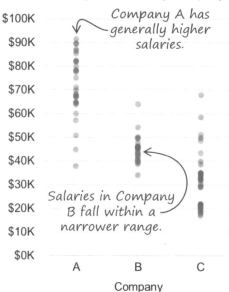

A "merged strip plot"

Employee Salaries by Company

Company A has generally higher salaries.

Salaries in Company B fall within a narrower range.

I use merged strip plots often because, compared with other chart types that we'll see in a moment, merged strip plots are the easiest for audiences to understand. The strip plot above, for example, can be explained to most audiences with a single sentence, such as: "Each dot represents the salary of one employee in each company." Another advantage of strip plots is that, as we saw in the previous section, they show individual values, which allows the audience to see outliers, clusters, gaps, and other distribution-related patterns more clearly than in "bin-based" charts like histograms.

As we also saw in the previous section, strip plots have their limitations: They don't show the overall shape of each distribution very well, and they don't allow the number of values in each bin (e.g., in each salary range) to be perceived or compared easily. They can also turn into mean-ingless solid lines of overlapping dots if there are lots of values, in which case you could use…

Merged jittered strip plots

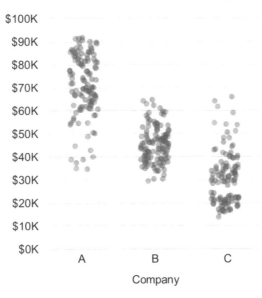

Key takeaway: Merged strip plots and merged jittered strip plots

- When comparing the distributions of multiple sets of values, consider using merged strip plots or merged jittered strip plots if it's more important to show individual values (gaps, clusters, outliers, etc.) than to show the overall shape of distributions or to compare the number of values in bins.

What if the sets of values that you want to visualize contain thousands of values (or more)? As we saw in the previous section, jittered strip plots can turn into meaningless blocks of overlapping dots when there are that many values, which is why we switched to a histogram in those cases. Can you use histograms to show multiple sets of values? Yes, you can, using...

Merged histograms

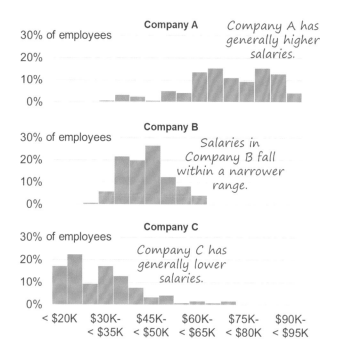

This chart works, but it's a bit tough to compare the bar heights among histograms (i.e., among different companies) since they're each in separate charts. There is, however, a clever hack that allows histograms to be compared more precisely, called...

Overlapping histograms

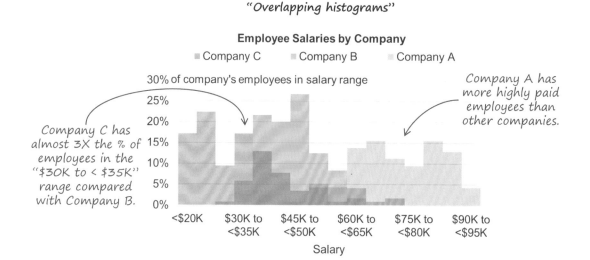

Making the histograms semitransparent and then overlapping them allows the audience to compare the bar lengths among different histograms very precisely.

> **Key takeaway: Overlapping histograms**
>
> • Consider using an overlapping histogram when showing the overall shapes of distributions or comparing the number of values in bins is more important than showing individual values (gaps, clusters, outliers, etc.).

Like all chart types, overlapping histograms have their downsides: They're harder to understand than merged strip plots, and they can start to look very visually busy if there are more than two or three sets of values (i.e., more than two or three histograms) in them:

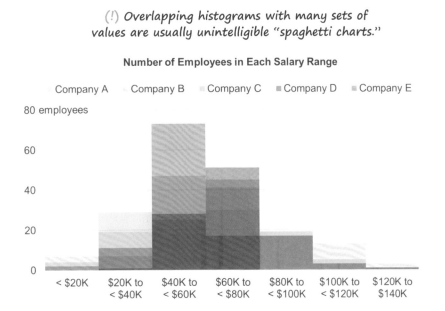

(!) Overlapping histograms with many sets of values are usually unintelligible "spaghetti charts."

If you find that an overlapping histogram of your data looks too busy, you could try…

Distribution line charts

A distribution line chart (or, in more jargony terms, a "frequency polygon") is basically an overlapping histogram that's been converted from a bar chart to a line chart:

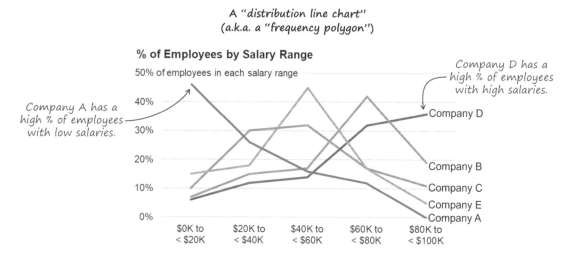

A "distribution line chart"
(a.k.a. a "frequency polygon")

% of Employees by Salary Range

Switching from bars to lines allows you to show more sets of values before the chart becomes too busy looking. How many sets of values (i.e., how many lines) can you show in a distribution line chart? Well, in *Practical Charts*, we saw a variety of ways to show up to 10, 15, or even 50 lines in a line chart, using tricks like stacked line charts and heatmaps. Those same tricks can be used with frequency polygons, as well.

You might also recall that, in *Practical Charts*, I warned against using line charts with scales other than time, and the horizontal scale in a distribution line chart definitely *isn't* time (it's salary bins in the example above). The reason why I included that warning in *Practical Charts* was because that book assumes that the audience has an *average* level of data savviness, and those audiences tend to get confused if the scale in a line chart isn't time. If, however, your audience has *above-average* levels of data savviness (as this book assumes), the risk that they'll get confused by a non-time line chart is lower, so distribution line charts become a viable option.

If you're worried that your audience will get confused by a non-time line chart but you think that they'll probably grasp histograms, you could switch back to a merged histogram to show a large number of sets of values:

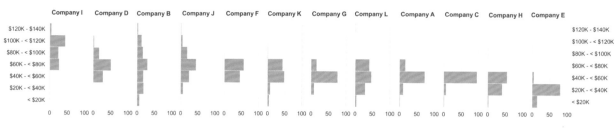

Merged histograms can show many sets of values and
may be less confusing than distribution line charts, but...

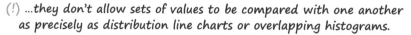

(!) ...they don't allow sets of values to be compared with one another
as precisely as distribution line charts or overlapping histograms.

Merged histograms pose a lower risk of confusing the audience than distribution line charts do, but, as we saw earlier, merged histograms also don't allow for precise comparisons of sets of values: If you want the audience to compare the length of a bar in one histogram with the length of a bar in another histogram in the chart, that will be trickier because they don't overlap like the lines in a distribution line chart do.

> **Key takeaways: Distribution line charts**
>
> • Consider using a distribution line chart when an overlapping histogram is too busy looking.
> • If the audience might get confused by a distribution line chart and high–precision comparison of bin counts isn't required, consider using a merged histogram instead.

There's another, lesser-known way to compare the distributions of multiple sets of values called…

Distribution heatmaps

A "distribution heatmap"

Employee Salary Distribution by Company

There's a wide range of employee salaries in Company B.

Most employees in Company C make $40K to < $60K.

I don't see distribution heatmaps much in the wild, but I use them all the time, mostly because audiences seem to find them easier to understand than merged histograms or distribution line charts. This could be because the darker color shades look more "dense," as if they contain higher concentrations of values, which they do.

Like all chart types, distribution heatmaps have their weaknesses, the main one being that they're not as *precise* as merged histograms or distribution line charts. Like all heatmaps, estimating the values in a distribution heatmap requires the audience to compare color shades in the chart with color shades in the legend, which only allows for rough estimates of values in the chart.

> **Key takeaways: Distribution heatmaps**
>
> - Consider using a distribution heatmap when the target audience may have trouble grasping merged histograms or distribution line charts.
> - Distribution heatmaps aren't as precise as merged histograms or distribution line charts.

> What about box plots? Why haven't you talked about those yet?

Box plots (not recommended)

There's another chart type that's often used to compare the distributions of multiple sets of values: a "box plot" or "box-and-whisker plot":

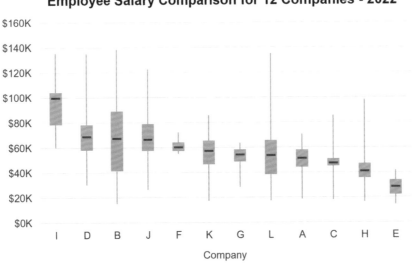

If you're unfamiliar with box plots, visit practicalreporting.com/pc-resources and click "Box plot explanation video" to learn how to read this chart type. I decided not to include that explanation in this book for two reasons:

1. It would require several pages to explain a box plot properly to someone who's not familiar with them or with concepts such as quartiles, which must be explained before explaining box plots.

2. After using box plots and teaching others how to use them for many years, I gradually came to believe that they're virtually never a better choice than other types of distribution charts, such as those that we've seen in this chapter, so I no longer recommend using them.

IMHO, box plots have fundamental design problems that make them unnecessarily hard to understand and prone to misinterpretation, even for expert chart readers. If you'd like to know more about why I came to this conclusion, visit practicalreporting.com/pc-resources, and click "I've stopped using box plots. Should you?" for a detailed article on this topic (and let me know on social media if you disagree with it!).

I realize that I'm taking a controversial position here because box plots have been in widespread use since the 1950s and are ubiquitous in certain domains, especially in research. If you work in one of those domains, you might get pushback if you suggest switching from box plots to another chart type. Although it's important to consider what the audience is used to seeing when choosing a chart type, it might also be worth at least trying to sell the audience on alternative chart types that could be more useful to them. "The chart type that people are used to seeing" isn't the same thing as "the most effective chart type for this situation." If you're being asked to use box plots (and if you agree with my arguments against using them), I'll leave it to you to decide whether to try to sell your audience on other chart types, or to continue to give them the box plots they (sadly) demand.

Key takeaway: Box plots

- I don't recommend using box plots because they're harder to grasp and more prone to misinterpretation than alternative chart types, such as merged histograms, distribution line charts, and distribution heatmaps, which can show the same insights as box plots.

As I mentioned in the introductory part of this book, there are plenty of other chart types beyond the 50 or so that I cover in *Practical Charts* and this book, and that's the case for distribution charts, as well. Other types of distribution charts that we didn't see include violin plots, bee swarm plots, and cumulative distribution charts. In my experience, these are useful in specialized domains or when doing advanced data analysis or mathematics, but they aren't usually needed for everyday charts.

As usual, let's summarize what we've learned in this section in a handy…

DECISION TREE:
CHOOSING A CHART TYPE TO COMPARE HOW MULTIPLE SETS OF VALUES ARE DISTRIBUTED

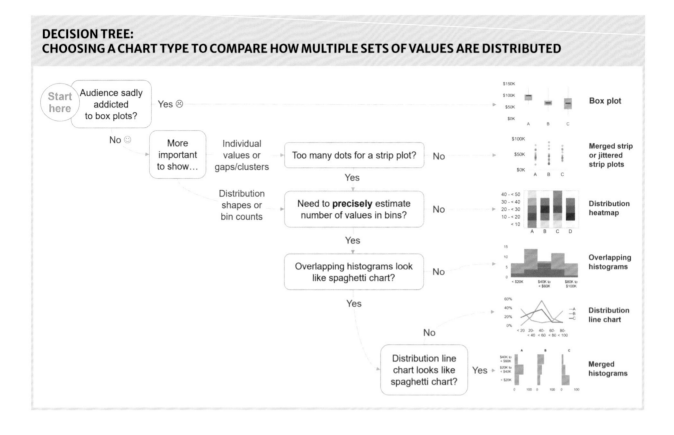

You've probably noticed that the scales of bin-based charts like histograms, distribution heatmaps, and distribution line charts look a little different than the quantitative scales that we saw in *Practical Charts*. That's because those chart types all have *interval scales*, which are quantitative scales that have been subdivided into *ranges*:

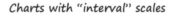

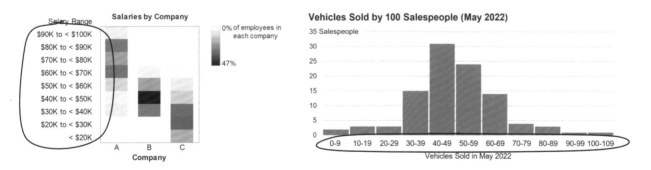

Like quantitative scales, there's a surprisingly large number of ways to screw up interval scales, so we should probably talk a bit about…

FORMATTING INTERVAL SCALES

Let's say you're conducting a study to see how long people can hold their breath, so you recruit 100 volunteers and time them. You want to get a sense of what those 100 volunteers' times were, and you decide to create a histogram. As with all bin-based charts, the histogram has an interval scale:

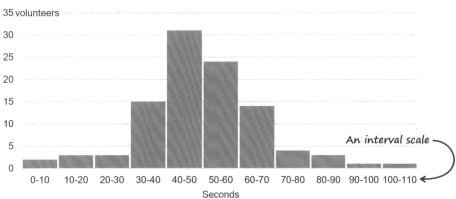

This chart shows many interesting insights, such as the fact that most volunteers are clustered in or around the "40–50 seconds" range. Note that there's nothing magical about intervals of 10; you could have also grouped volunteers into intervals of 5 seconds or 20 seconds, as we saw in the "How many bins should my histogram have?" section.

> **Key takeaways: Interval scales**
>
> • Interval scales are quantitative scales that have been subdivided into equal (or essentially equal) sub-ranges.
> • Interval scales are often useful in distribution charts but are often poorly designed.

Although the interval scale in the chart above is useful, it has some problems that should be fixed before it's published. Let's start by asking whatever dataviz software product we're using to create an interval scale from scratch, based on the "breath-holding times" data:

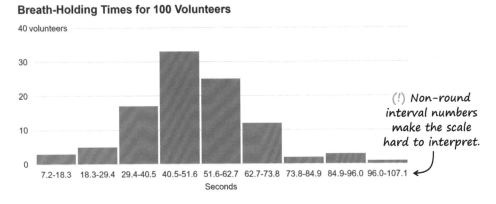

Breath-Holding Times for 100 Volunteers

40 volunteers

(!) Non-round interval numbers make the scale hard to interpret.

Seconds

Wow. That's pretty bad. It's also your first key takeaway regarding interval scales: Unfortunately, **many dataviz software products generate poorly formatted interval scales by default,** and you usually need to fix them before publishing a chart that includes them.

Let's at least tweak the intervals so that they're round numbers:

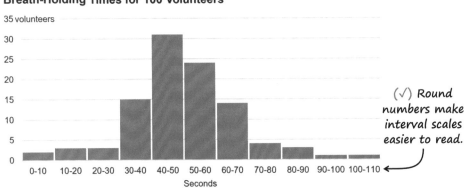

Breath-Holding Times for 100 Volunteers

35 volunteers

(✓) Round numbers make interval scales easier to read.

Seconds

Aaaah… Much easier to read now. Finding intervals that result in round numbers can require a bit of trial and error, and changing the intervals changes the chart (i.e., the number of bars and the lengths of the bars are now a bit different), but this version of the chart still represents the data accurately.

Key takeaways: Round numbers in interval scales

- Try to create interval scales with round numbers.
- Most dataviz software products don't generate interval scales with round numbers by default, so interval scales often need to be edited to use round numbers before being published.

There's a new problem with this edited scale, though: Let's say one of the volunteers had a breath-holding time of 10 seconds. Would they be counted in the "0–10 seconds" interval or the "10–20 seconds" interval?

Uh-oh.

As it turns out, the intervals in the chart above *overlap*. This is a problem because it's not clear in which interval times such as 10 seconds, 20 seconds, or 30 seconds should go. The solution? Make sure that the intervals in your interval scales *don't overlap:*

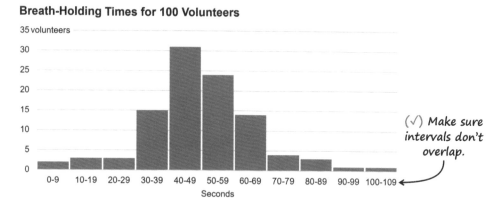

There we go. Now there's only *one* interval in which a time of 10 seconds could be counted (the "10–19 seconds" interval).

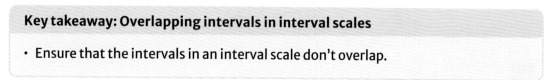

Key takeaway: Overlapping intervals in interval scales

• Ensure that the intervals in an interval scale don't overlap.

The interval scale in the chart above works fine if you're measuring times in seconds, but what if you had used a more accurate stopwatch and recorded times in *tenths* of a second? In which interval would a time of, say, 19.5 seconds go? The "10-19" interval only includes times up to—but not over—19 seconds, and it definitely wouldn't go in the "20-29" interval. As it turns out, then, this interval scale now has *gaps* in it. How can you close the gaps? You can format the interval scale labels a little differently:

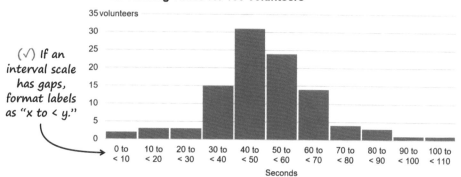

Ah! It's now clear that a time such as 19.5 seconds would go in the "10 to < 20" interval because that interval includes times up to (but not including) 20 seconds. Even if there were a time of 19.99999 seconds, it would still be clear in which interval it would be counted. I realize that this label formatting isn't as easy to read as "0-9, 10-19, 20-29, …" But as we just saw, that easier-to-read formatting doesn't allow the data to be represented correctly.

Now, it's important to note that, if the units in an interval scale were something like "transactions" instead of "seconds," you *could* use scale labels such as "0-9, 10-19, 20-29, …" Why? Because you can't have "19.5 transactions"; you can only have "19 transactions" or "20 transactions." Therefore, you don't have to worry about values "falling into gaps." FYI, units like transactions, employees, and vehicles that *can't* be subdivided into smaller units are called "discrete" units, while units like seconds, meters, feet, tons, etc., that *can* be subdivided into smaller units, are called "continuous" units.

Key takeaways: Formatting interval scale labels

- If the units of an interval scale are continuous units, consider formatting the scale labels as "x to < y."
- If the units of an interval scale are discrete units, consider formatting the scale labels as "x–y."

The interval scale in our "breath-holding times" chart is in much better shape now, but it looks like there's a ton of volunteers in the "40 to < 50 seconds" interval. Maybe it would be useful to split that interval into two smaller intervals so that we can show how many volunteers had times in the low 40s (40 to < 45 seconds) and how many had times in the high 40s (45 to < 50 seconds):

Breath-Holding Times for 100 Volunteers

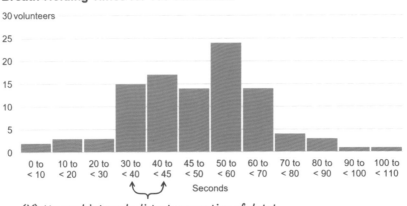

(X) Unequal intervals distort perception of data!

Although this version of the chart shows that there are slightly more volunteers who had times in the low 40s than times in the high 40s (which wasn't visible before), it *also* now looks like more volunteers had times in the 50s than any other range. That's *wrong*, though! There are far more volunteers who had times in the 40s than times in the 50s, *but this chart makes it look like that wasn't the case.* Making the intervals unequal misrepresented the data! To represent the data accurately, then, **all the intervals in an interval scale must be the same size**—for example, all intervals of 10 seconds.

Like any good guideline, there is, of course, an exception to this one: In the chart above, there are very few volunteers in the "80 to < 90," "90 to < 100," and "100 to < 110" intervals, but those three intervals are taking up a lot of room in this chart. They could be grouped into a single interval, though, like this:

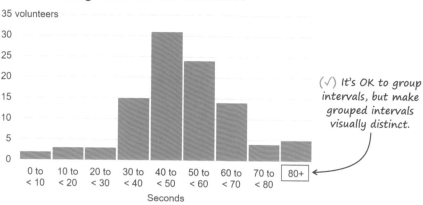

It's OK to group intervals like this, but there *is* a risk that the audience won't notice that one of the intervals is a different size than the others, so you *must* make labels for grouped intervals visually distinct from the other scale labels. In the example above, I put a box around the label for the grouped interval ("80+"), but you could bold the label or make it stand out in some other way.

> ### Key takeaways: Interval sizes
>
> - Generally, make all intervals in an interval scale the same size.
> - Intervals can be grouped to save space, but make the labels for grouped intervals visually distinct from the other scale labels so that the audience notices that grouped intervals aren't the same size as the others.

As usual, let's summarize what we saw in this section in a…

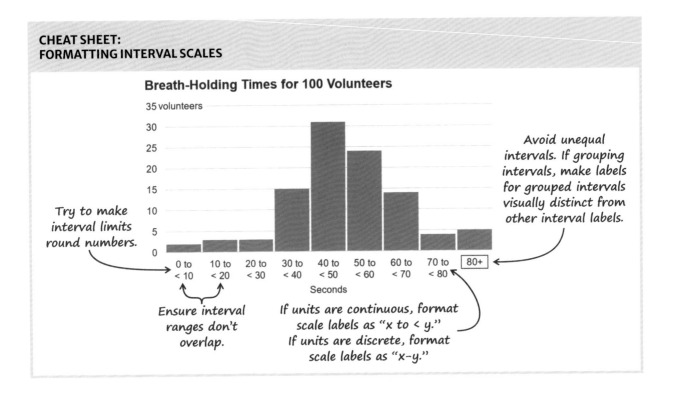

CHEAT SHEET:
FORMATTING INTERVAL SCALES

Breath-Holding Times for 100 Volunteers

Avoid unequal intervals. If grouping intervals, make labels for grouped intervals visually distinct from other interval labels.

Try to make interval limits round numbers.

Ensure interval ranges don't overlap.

If units are continuous, format scale labels as "x to < y." If units are discrete, format scale labels as "x-y."

Now that we've covered the main types of distribution charts, I want to mention a few…

USEFUL ENHANCEMENTS FOR DISTRIBUTION CHARTS

Three enhancements that I regularly add to distribution charts are:

- Showing means or medians
- Combining different distribution chart types
- Using inset charts

Let's have a quick look at each of these, beginning with…

Showing means or medians

When showing distributions, it's often useful to include means or *medians*. For those who need a refresher from secondary school, the "median of a set of values" is the point at which half the values fall above that point and half the values fall below. For example, the median salary of a company would be the salary at which half the employees make less than that salary and half make more.

Medians or means can be added to any of the distribution chart types that we've seen:

Combining distribution chart types

It's possible to combine different distribution chart types into a single chart, for example, to combine a histogram with a strip plot or a distribution heatmap with a strip plot:

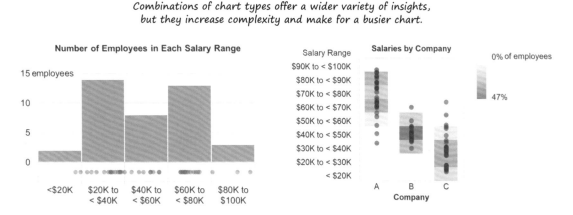

It's tempting to combine chart types like this because the combination makes a wider variety of insights visible, but additional chart types also add complexity for the audience. In my experience, that additional complexity isn't needed in most cases. A single chart type is usually able to say what you need to say about the data, although there are rare times when what you need to say can't be communicated with a single chart type, so the additional complexity of showing multiple chart types is warranted.

Inset charts (in distribution charts)

What if there are outliers in your distribution data that "crush" the other values in a distribution chart?

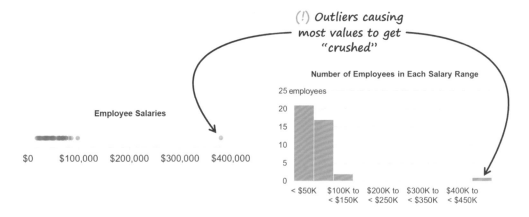

We already saw the solution to this challenge in *Practical Charts*, so this is just a reminder that you can use inset charts with distribution charts, as well as most other chart types:

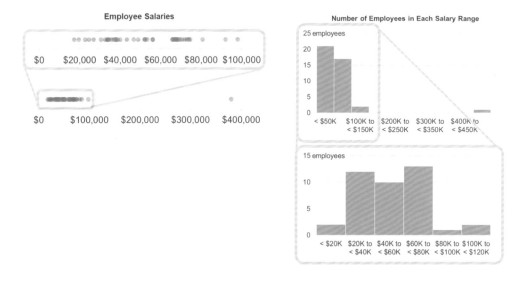

Before we leave distribution charts behind, I want to mention a distribution-related problem that I see all the time in practice, and that has to do with…

SHOWING DISTRIBUTIONS CHANGING OVER TIME

Earlier in this chapter, we saw that, when showing averages, it's important to show distribution charts along with those averages. **This also applies to showing averages changing over time.** For example, let's say that you create a line chart of your company's average monthly customer satisfaction rating for the past 12 months, and it looks like this:

Not much going on here, right? Looks like customer satisfaction was pretty steady throughout the year. Just for giggles, though, let's layer on the distributions of those monthly averages as a distribution heatmap:

Whoa! As it turns out, a major change occurred during this year. In July, customers suddenly split into a group of extremely satisfied ones and a group of dissatisfied ones, but the "average" line made it look like nothing happened. Imagine if the audience only saw the "average" line without *also* seeing a graph of how the *distribution* of satisfaction ratings changed over time!

Unfortunately, showing distributions changing over time is rarely done in practice, which has resulted in many "average over time" charts that have led to countless bad decisions.

A quick formatting note about distribution heatmaps: You might have noticed that I removed the gaps between the columns of colored cells (i.e., between the months) in the heatmap above. This is because the categories in this chart (months) are *sequential*, and, in my experience, audiences find it more intuitive to see distribution heatmaps of sequential categories with the gaps removed, probably because it makes the heatmap look more like a sequence of colored cells rather than a set of discrete stacks of colored cells. You can, as always, decide if you want to follow this convention or not.

Also note that I could have used other chart types that we saw in this chapter to show distributions changing over time:

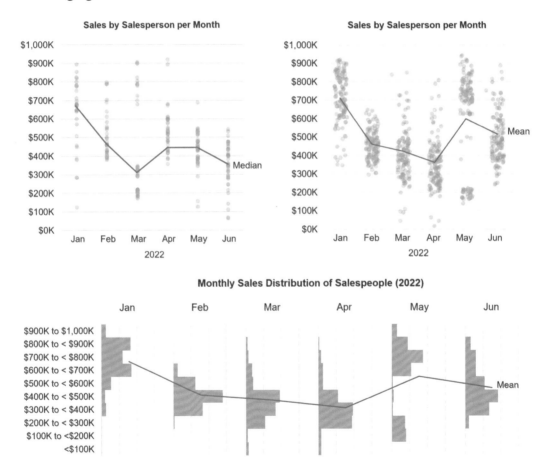

Which of these chart types should you choose when you need to show a distribution changing over time? Each time period (each month, in the above examples) is just a set of values, so the

"Choosing a chart type to compare how multiple sets of values are distributed" decision tree that we saw earlier can be used to choose a chart type for showing distributions changing over time.

> **Key takeaway: Showing averages and distributions changing over time**
>
> - When showing averages changing over time, consider also showing distribution charts along with those averages.

OK, that (finally) does it for charts for showing how values are distributed across a range. Now that you know how to design these chart types effectively and how powerful they can be, I suspect that you might find yourself using them often, if you weren't already.

On to the final family of chart types that we'll cover in this book, which are chart types for…

Chapter 5

Showing how variables are related

LET'S SAY THAT you work for a charitable organization that raises donations over the phone from a call center that employs 32 call center agents. The organization tracks several metrics for each agent, including the number of hours of training that they've received and the average donation amount that they raise per work shift:

Agent Name	Hours of Training	Avg. Donations Raised/Shift
Cameron O.	3.0	$1,406
Tara J.	3.5	$975
Rajesh S.	3.5	$1,423
Frank L.	4.3	$1,709
Jim B.	5.0	$1,994
Laura K.	5.8	$1,798
Heidi O.	6.0	$1,918
Maria G.	6.0	$1,857
Son L.	6.5	$1,476
Laura J.	6.5	$2,138
Jose R.	7.5	$2,336
Tiffany P.	8.0	$2,999
Shaun R.	8.8	$2,696
Todd H.	9.3	$2,450
Penelope A.	9.5	$2,525
Adriana E.	9.8	$2,550
Lucy. L.	10.0	$2,186
Kate B.	11.0	$2,613
LaShonda R.	11.4	$2,519
Jeff L.	11.7	$2,801
Theo B.	12.8	$2,931
Tina J.	12.8	$4,571
Jennifer B.	13.3	$3,505
Sarah F.	13.3	$4,121
Catherine M.	13.5	$4,545
Percy I.	14.8	$5,077
Nicole E.	14.8	$3,755
Julie R.	15.8	$3,660
Sarah Q.	16.0	$2,841
Sergei R.	17.0	$4,250
Javi L.	19.0	$4,588
Valentina M.	19.5	$5,528

Unsurprisingly, the management team wants to know if agents with more training raise more in donations. That question isn't easy to answer based on the table above, but it becomes obvious if this data is shown as…

MERGED BAR CHARTS (FOR SHOWING CORRELATION)

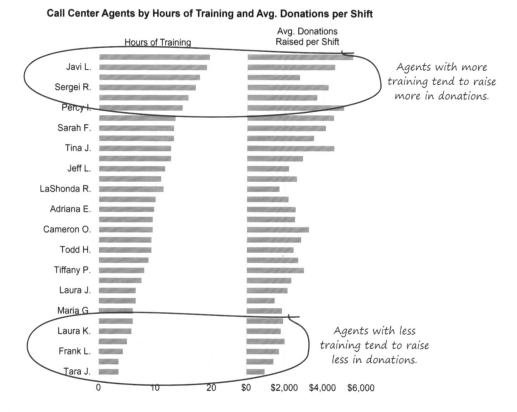

A "merged bar chart" for showing correlation

Call Center Agents by Hours of Training and Avg. Donations per Shift

Agents with more training tend to raise more in donations.

Agents with less training tend to raise less in donations.

This chart clearly answers the management team's question: Agents who've had more training do, indeed, generally tend to raise more in donations.

Obviously, a chart like this is pretty useful, but it comes with a note of caution: When shown the chart above, many audiences will interpret it to mean that more training *causes* agents to raise more in donations and that, for example, giving agents more training will increase donations. While that *might* be true, it might not be.

What? Why not?

Well, it could be that agents who are more *enthusiastic* tend to raise more in donations and also tend to sign up for more training sessions. If that were the case, it would be agents' *higher enthusiasm* that was causing them to raise more in donations, not their higher number of hours of training. In fact, there could be all sorts of reasons why agents with more training tend to raise more in donations, and more investigation would be needed to determine what, exactly, is causing what. What the chart above does show is that there's a *relationship* between "Hours of

Training" and "Donations Raised per Shift," that is, that these two variables are *correlated* in a certain way, which can be very useful to know, even if it isn't yet known *why* they're correlated.

Of course, there are all sorts of different correlation relationships that we might have seen in this data, for example:

Note that, in merged bar charts like these, it's important to put the variable that you think might be *causing* the other variable's change (a.k.a. the "independent variable") in the first column, and the variable that might be *being changed* (a.k.a. the "dependent variable") in the second column, and then sort both columns by the variable in the first column. For example, it seems likelier that more training would cause agents to raise more donations than that more donations would cause agents to receive more training, so the first column of bars should be "Hours of Training" and the agents should be sorted by "Hours of Training" in both columns of bars. If you're not sure what might be causing what, just pick a variable at random to put in the first column.

As we've seen, merged bar charts can be useful for all sorts of things and "showing if and how variables are related" can now be added to that list.

> **Key takeaways: Using merged bar charts to show if/how variables are related**
>
> - If you need to show if/how two variables are related, consider using a merged bar chart.
> - In a "correlation" merged bar chart, put the independent variable in the first column of bars and sort both columns of bars by the independent variable.

In addition to merged bars, there are other chart types for showing if or how variables are related, the most notable being...

SCATTER PLOTS

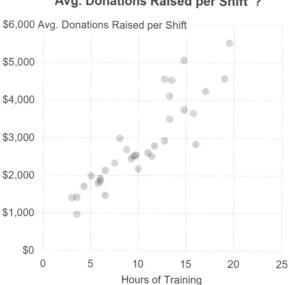

A "scatter plot"

Is "Hours of Training" related to
"Avg. Donations Raised per Shift"?

If you're not sure how to read a scatter plot (a.k.a. a "scatterplot" or "scatter chart"), let me explain: The scatter plot above shows the same call center agent data that we saw in the previous section, with each dot representing one call center agent (so, 32 dots). Each dot's vertical position represents the donations raised per shift for that agent, and its horizontal position represents the number of hours of training for that agent:

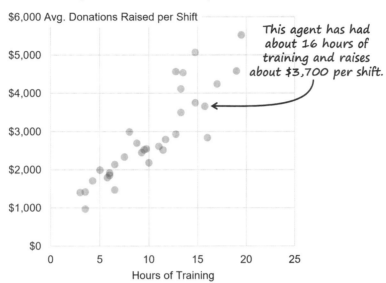

Note that, like strip plots, it's important to make the dots in a scatter plot semitransparent so that the audience can see if there are overlapping dots in the same location (e.g., multiple agents who have the same Hours of Training and Average Donations Raised per Shift).

The dots in a scatter plot often form a *pattern*, and that pattern is what tells you if or how the two variables in the chart are related:

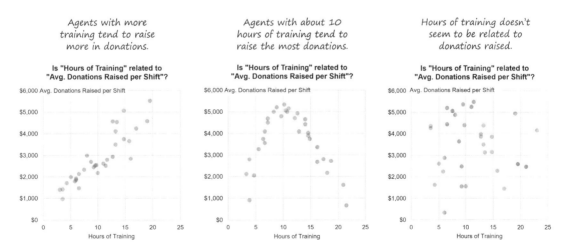

While very useful, scatter plots are a bit more complex than merged bar charts and can be hard for some audiences to grasp.

If scatter plots can be harder to grasp than merged bar charts, why not always use merged bar charts instead to show how variables are related?

Scatter plots have three important advantages over merged bar charts:

1. Certain types of relationships are clearer in scatter plots than in merged bar charts.

Have a look at the merged bar chart below:

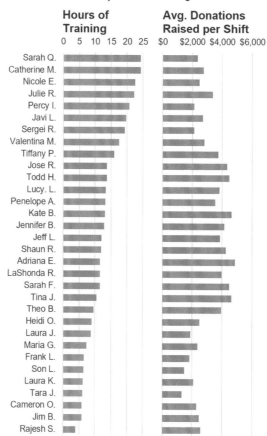

Hmm. There seems to be *some* sort of relationship here, but it's hard to tell exactly what it is. What if the same data was shown as a scatter plot?

Huh! The scatter plot makes it immediately clear that there are three distinct "clusters" of agents with different levels of donations and training hours. That wasn't as clear in the merged bar chart, though. As it turns out, then, simple relationships are usually clear in both merged bar charts and scatter plots, but **more complex relationships** (like the "three cluster" one above) **might only be clear in a scatter plot.** Therefore, if the relationship that you need to feature is more complex, you might need to use a scatter plot to communicate it to your audience. This also means that, when looking for correlations yourself (as opposed to showing insights to an audience), you should always look at the data as a scatter plot to make sure that you're not missing patterns that wouldn't be as clear in a merged bar chart.

2. Scatter plots can show more values than merged bar charts.

Merged bar charts work well with up to about 50 pairs of values, but you can probably imagine what a merged bar chart with 100 or 500 pairs of bars would look like (i.e., very visually busy).

Scatter plots, however, are usually still easy to interpret with hundreds or even thousands of dots. If a scatter plot becomes too visually busy, there are special types of scatter plots such as "density plots" that can show patterns among virtually any number of values:

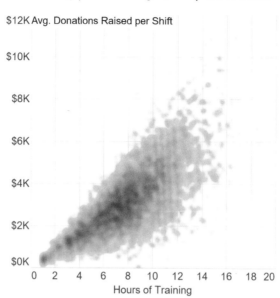

A "density plot" showing 5,000 pairs of values

3. Scatter plots can show features, such as trendlines, that summarize relationships.

Most dataviz software products allow chart creators to add a *trendline* to a scatter plot with one click:

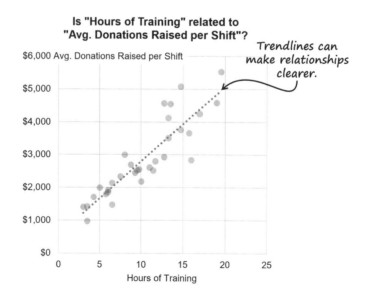

Trendlines "summarize" the pattern of dots, which can be useful to clarify the relationship between two variables, but "correlation summarization" trendlines can't be added to merged bar charts.

If you decide to add a trendline to a scatter plot, though, *be careful*. For example, most dataviz software products will happily add a trendline even when the dots *don't* form a discernable pattern:

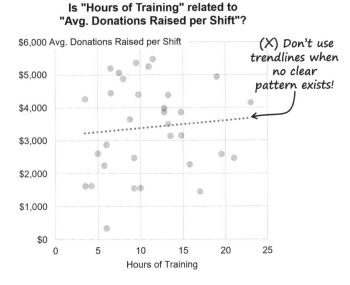

This can suggest that two variables are related when, in fact, they might not be related at all.

It's also important to be aware that some dot patterns aren't well-summarized by linear (straight) trendlines:

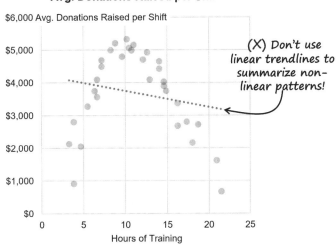

There are more complex types of trendlines, such as polynomial trendlines, that can be used to summarize nonlinear patterns like the one above, but those are advanced data analysis techniques that are unlikely to be needed for everyday reports and presentations, and therefore fall outside the scope of this book.

Key takeaways: Trendlines in scatter plots

- Relationship summarization features such as trendlines can be added to scatter plots, but generally not to merged bar charts.
- Adding trendlines to scatter plots can make relationship patterns clearer.
- Avoid adding trendlines when no clear dot pattern is visible, and avoid adding linear trendlines when the dot pattern isn't linear.

Despite these advantages of scatter plots, I still recommend defaulting to merged bar charts to show how two variables are related because merged bar charts are generally easier to read. I'd only switch to a scatter plot when a merged bar chart looks overly busy or doesn't make the insight(s) that you need to feature clear.

> What if I need to use a scatter plot for one of those reasons, but I'm worried that my audience will struggle to understand how to read it?

In that case, you could try using the tricks that we saw in *Practical Charts* for explaining chart types that might be unfamiliar to an audience:

Gentle reveal:

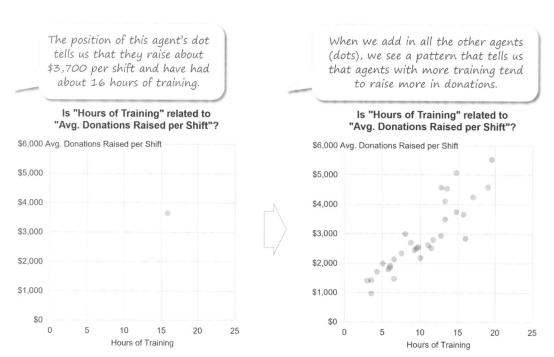

Bait and switch:

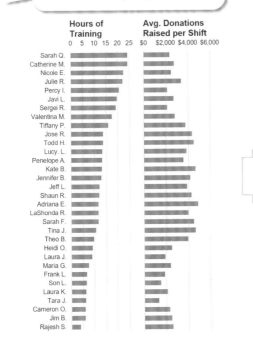

Duh insights:

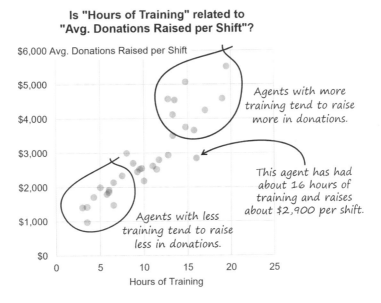

Key takeaways: Using scatter plots to show if/how variables are related

- By default, consider using merged bar charts to show if/how variables are related.
- Consider using a scatter plot when the relationship to be featured isn't clear in a merged bar chart, when there are too many values for a merged bar chart, or when relationship summarization features (e.g., trendlines) need to be shown.
- If there's a risk that your audience will struggle to understand how to read a scatter plot, use the "gentle reveal," "bait and switch," and/or "duh insights" tricks to help them learn how to read it.

As you can see, correlation charts such as merged bar charts and scatter plots can be very useful, but many organizations don't use them often or, sometimes, at all. If you weren't using them before, you might find yourself using them regularly now that you have an idea of the powerful kinds of insights that they can show.

Before recapping what we've learned about correlation charts, I want to mention a challenge that often comes up in practice, which is...

SHOWING DIFFERENT CATEGORIES OF ITEMS

Let's say that, in the chart of call center agents, it was necessary to distinguish among full-time, part-time, and contract call center agents. Generally, the most effective way to identify different categories of items is to use different colors:

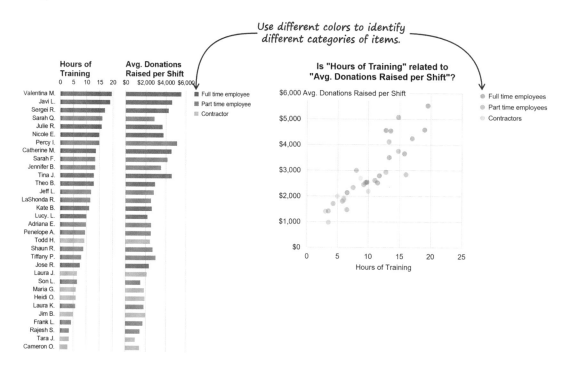

> ### Key takeaway: Identifying categories of items in correlation charts
>
> - To identify different categories of items in correlation charts, consider using different colors.

We've covered a lot in this chapter, so now's probably a good time to take a breather and recap the guidelines that we've learned so far, as well as a few other minor guidelines, in a couple of cheat sheets:

CHEAT SHEET:
FORMATTING MERGED BAR CHARTS FOR SHOWING CORRELATION

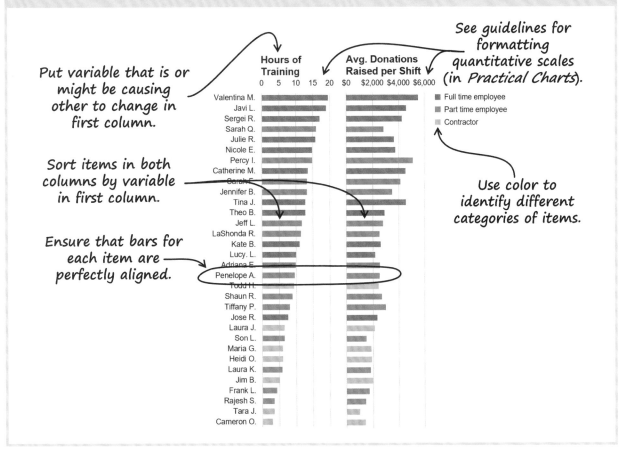

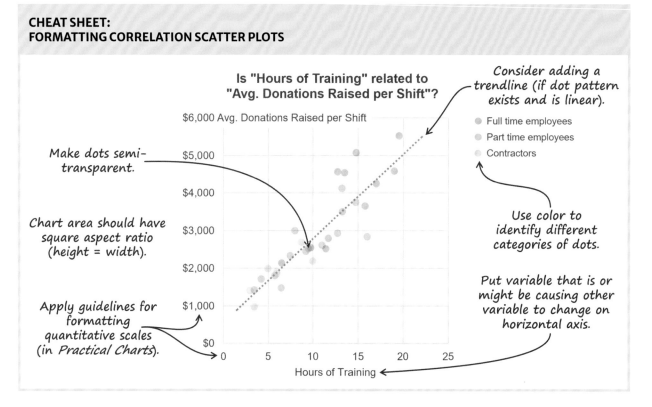

CHEAT SHEET:
FORMATTING CORRELATION SCATTER PLOTS

In many cases, the relationship between variables isn't set in stone and can change over time, so it's possible that you might find yourself needing to show how a correlation changed over time in a chart. TBH, you probably won't need to do this very often, but just in case it comes up, here are some ways of…

SHOWING CORRELATIONS CHANGING OVER TIME

There are two types of challenges here, depending on whether…

1. Each period of time (each day, each month, etc.) has *one* pair of values associated with it, or…

2. Each period of time has *more than one* pair of values associated with it.

Let's look at the first possibility, in which each time period has one pair of values associated with it. In the data set below, for example, each day has one pair of values associated with it:

Online Ad Spend and Website Visits
Jan. 1 to Feb. 29, 2020

Date	Online Ad Spend ($)	Website Visits
1-Jan-2020	243	60,359
2-Jan-2020	206	69,582
3-Jan-2020	299	82,445
4-Jan-2020	144	36,357
5-Jan-2020	171	48,789
6-Jan-2020	241	58,365
7-Jan-2020	196	40,398
8-Jan-2020	334	48,221
9-Jan-2020	333	118,584
10-Jan-2020	288	110,069

If this data set contained values for 60 days, it might look like this as a scatter plot:

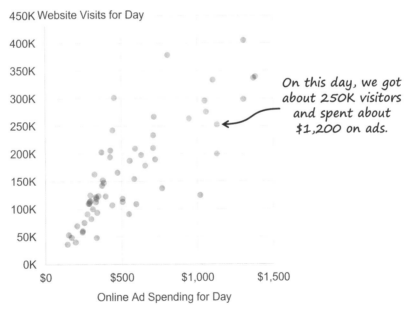

In a chart like this, *some* types of insights are clear, such as the fact that days with lower ad spending tended to also have fewer website visits. What *isn't* clear, however, is how these variables relate to each other *over time*. Did ad spending or website visits increase over time, or decrease? Did the two variables have similar patterns of change? Hmmm…

One solution in these situations is to connect each point in time (i.e., each dot) to the next point in time with a line, which produces a *connected scatter plot:*

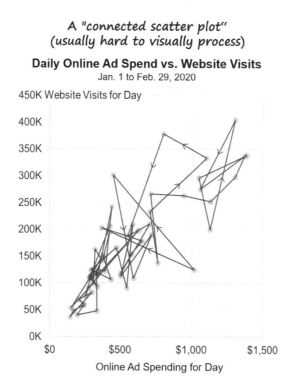

A "connected scatter plot"
(usually hard to visually process)

Daily Online Ad Spend vs. Website Visits
Jan. 1 to Feb. 29, 2020

In theory, this shows how these values changed over time. In practice, however, this chart type often results in a spaghetti chart like the one above. Opinions differ in the dataviz community on the usefulness of connected scatter plots: Many believe that they can be effective in specific situations, however, I think that other chart types are virtually always a better choice, even in those situations. You can, of course, decide for yourself, but if you want to read more about why I don't recommend using connected scatter plots for everyday charts, visit practicalreporting.com/pc-resources and click "About connected scatter plots."

> If you don't recommend connected scatter plots, what are the "other chart types" that you mentioned for showing how the relationship between two variables changed over time?

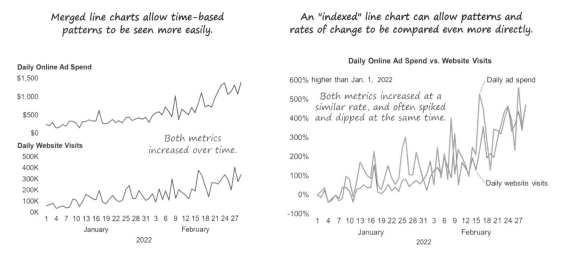

Merged line charts allow time-based patterns to be seen more easily.

An "indexed" line chart can allow patterns and rates of change to be compared even more directly.

Now, let's look at the second possibility, in which each period of time has *more than one* pair of values associated with it. In the scenario below, each month has *multiple* pairs of values associated with it:

Transaction Values and Discounts by Month (2022)

January		February		March		April		May	
Transaction Value	Discount %	Transaction Value	Discount %	Transaction Value	Discount %	Transaction Value	Discount %	Transaction Value	Discount %
$32,552	1.2%	$275,112	1.0%	$235,885	2.1%	$138,851	4.2%	$538,512	6.2%
$28,442	1.9%	$38,125	2.5%	$38,125	6.2%	$188,521	4.5%	$208,821	8.0%
$168,552	4.0%	$175,221	2.5%	$175,221	7.5%	$248,155	5.8%	$345,112	8.3%
$75,112	5.2%	$248,112	2.5%	$278,552	7.5%	$199,852	6.6%	$98,552	8.3%
$37,152	6.4%	$168,552	5.0%	$168,552	9.3%	$299,885	6.9%	$78,552	8.5%
$188,552	6.9%	$98,122	5.0%	$98,122	11.1%	$188,552	7.0%	$238,890	9.1%
$78,552	7.4%	$177,885	5.9%	$177,885	11.5%	$388,715	8.0%	$159,750	10.2%
$168,552	9.1%	$104,223	7.3%	$104,223	5.9%	$168,552	9.0%	$184,020	10.7%
$98,122	11.1%	$114,452	7.7%	$114,452	6.0%	$98,122	9.2%	$301,225	11.2%
$58,442	11.3%	$158,875	9.4%	$312,552	8.1%	$398,881	9.5%	$249,580	11.5%
$104,223	11.5%	$125,882	9.5%	$125,882	9.0%	$104,223	11.0%	$385,319	11.9%
$114,452	12.0%	$253,442	11.0%	$253,442	10.6%	$568,842	11.8%	$278,851	12.2%
$158,875	13.0%	$224,112	11.1%	$224,112	11.2%	$158,875	12.1%	$278,556	12.4%
$125,882	14.1%	$172,005	13.1%	$172,005	12.4%	$125,882	12.5%	$523,442	12.7%
$253,442	14.9%	$279,996	14.0%	$279,996	13.8%	$253,442	13.1%	$189,716	12.7%
$224,112	15.2%	$298,554	14.5%	$298,554	13.9%	$35,112	14.7%	$201,552	13.2%
$172,005	15.6%	$348,851	14.9%	$348,851	13.9%	$178,221	18.4%	$348,201	13.4%
$279,996	15.7%	$378,855	15.5%	$378,855	14.9%	$298,852	19.1%	$438,112	13.5%
$298,554	16.6%	$475,125	16.1%	$475,125	15.4%	$348,851	21.7%	$399,885	16.0%
$348,851	17.5%	$248,851	17.8%	$248,851	15.6%	$388,884	23.0%	$344,900	16.2%
$378,855	22.5%	$348,851	19.0%	$348,851	16.0%			$127,112	17.4%
$475,125	25.0%	$175,123	22.5%	$422,445	17.2%				
$248,851	25.0%	$502,554	25.0%	$502,554	19.8%				
$348,851	27.2%			$128,556	27.1%				

With data like this, you could show one scatter plot for each period of time (e.g., one scatter plot per month), but it's not easy to see how the scatter plots change from one period to the next:

Tricky to see how these changed from one month to the next

Probably the best that you'll be able to do in a situation like this is to summarize the correlation for each time period as a trendline and show how that trendline changed over time:

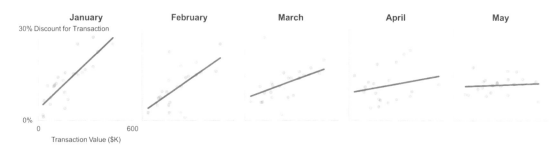

Key takeaways: Showing the relationship between two variables over time

- When the data contains one pair of values per time period, line charts are generally better options than scatter plots for showing how two variables are related over time.
- When the data consists of more than one pair of values per time period, consider showing it as multiple scatter plots with trendlines.

In all the scenarios we've seen so far in this chapter, we needed to show how *two* variables were related to each other. In practice, though, you might find yourself needing show how *more than two* variables are related to one another, so let's talk about…

SHOWING RELATIONSHIPS AMONG THREE VARIABLES

Let's modify the call center scenario that we saw earlier and assume that we now need to show relationships among Average Donations Raised per Shift, Hours of Training, and a *third* variable: Employee Satisfaction Rating. This third variable can be easily added as a third column of bars in…

Merged bar charts (for showing relationships among three variables)

A merged bar chart showing relationships among three variables

Note that the "Hours of Training" variable is in the first column of bars, and all the columns are sorted by Hours of Training. This is because I suspect that training is the main factor that's causing the other two variables to change. If, however, I suspected that Employee Satisfaction were the main factor that was causing higher donations and more hours of training, then I'd put "Employee Satisfaction" in the first column and sort the other columns by that variable.

> **Key takeaways: Merged bar charts for showing relationships among three variables**
>
> - To show if or how three variables are related to one another, consider using a merged bar chart.
> - As with any "correlation" merged bar chart, put the independent variable in the first column of bars and sort all columns by the variable in the first column.

As we saw earlier in this chapter, there are certain types of relationships that are clearer in scatter plots than in merged bar charts, so it might be useful to show three variables in a scatter plot. Is there a way? Yes. Two, in fact. The first way is to use…

"Colored-dot" scatter plots

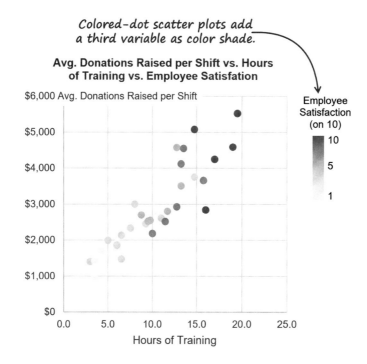

In the colored-dot scatter plot above, dots with a darker shade of blue represent agents with higher Employee Satisfaction ratings, allowing the chart to show relationships among three variables instead of just two. For example, the chart above shows that agents with high donation amounts and many hours of training (i.e., dots in the upper right of the chart) also tend to have high employee satisfaction (i.e., a darker shade of blue). Note that the audience will only be able to make rough estimates and comparisons of values that are shown as dot color (Employee Satisfaction values, in the example above) because, as we saw in the "Heatmaps" chapter, it's hard to compare color shades precisely.

Key takeaway: Colored-dot scatterplots for showing relationships among three variables

- If the relationships to be featured among three variables aren't clear in a merged bar chart, there are too many values to show in a merged bar chart, or relationship summarization features (e.g., trendlines) need to be shown, consider using a colored-dot scatter plot.

What if some of the dots overlap, though? Normally, you'd solve this problem by, as we saw earlier, making the dots semitransparent. You can't do that in a colored-dot scatter plot, though, because that would alter the colors of the dots and distort the audience's perception of the Employee Satisfaction values. If some dots overlap, then, you could switch to…

Bubble charts

A bubble chart is just a scatter plot with a third variable shown as *dot size:*

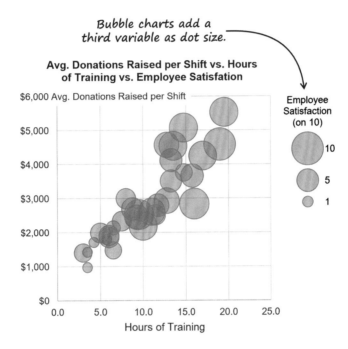

In the bubble chart above, larger dots represent agents with higher Employee Satisfaction ratings. This means it's also a "shape size chart," like those we saw in the "heatmaps" chapter. Conceptually, a bubble chart is similar to a colored-dot scatter plot, so insights that are clear in one will usually also be clear in the other. As with colored-dot scatter plots, the third variable in a bubble chart can only be estimated and compared roughly, since it's difficult to estimate and compare the sizes of bubbles precisely.

There are, however, a few minor differences between colored-dot scatter plots and bubble charts that might cause you to favor one or the other in a given situation:

- In my experience, audiences with lower levels of data savviness tend to find colored-dot scatter plots a bit more intuitive, except for variables that people think of as being physically bigger or smaller, such as land area, body mass, etc., in which case a bubble chart can seem more intuitive.

- Colored dots generally allow the variables on the vertical and horizontal axes to be estimated and compared a bit more precisely because it can be hard to eyeball the exact center of a large bubble in a bubble chart.

⊜ As I mentioned earlier, bubble charts do a better job of showing overlapping dots (as long as the bubbles are semitransparent and have borders, as in the example above).

In most situations, though, you won't go too wrong with either option; try both to see what works best in the situation at hand.

> **Key takeaway: Bubble charts for showing relationships among three variables**
>
> • If the relationships to be featured among three variables aren't clear in a merged bar chart, there are too many values to show in a merged bar chart, relationship summarization features (e.g., trendlines) need to be shown, or there are values that "overlap," consider using a bubble chart.

Now that we have some solutions for showing how three variables are related, let's keep pushing. How about…

SHOWING RELATIONSHIPS AMONG MORE THAN THREE VARIABLES

What if you needed to show how *more* than three variables are related to one another? Well, merged bar charts work just fine with four, five, or even more columns of bars:

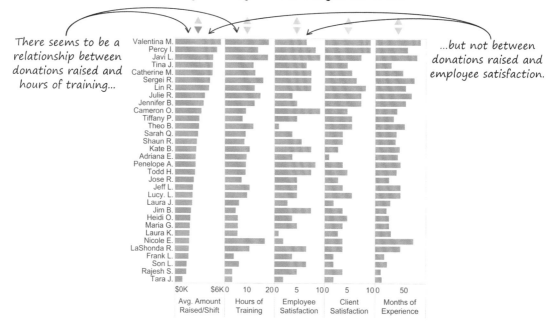

A "dynamically sortable merged bar chart"

There seems to be a relationship between donations raised and hours of training…

…but not between donations raised and employee satisfaction.

A chart like this can be particularly useful when *analyzing* data yourself. If you try sorting the chart by different variables (i.e., by different columns of bars), you can often spot potentially useful relationships among variables. A chart like this might, however, be too complex for some audiences, and you might decide to just use it yourself to find relationships among variables and then communicate those relationships as simpler charts or bullet points on a slide or in a report.

What about scatter plots? Is there a way to use those to show relationships among more than three variables? Yes, you could use a *scatter plot matrix:*

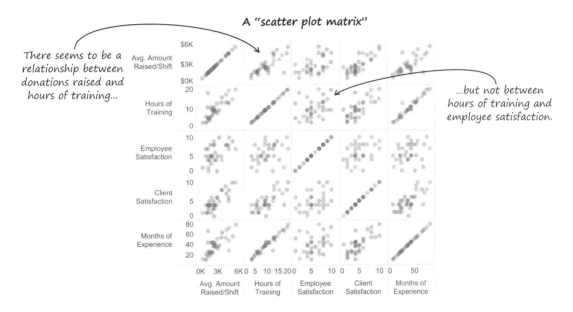

This is obviously more complex-looking than a merged bar chart but, as we've seen, some types of relationships are clearer in scatter plots than merged bars, so I recommend always viewing the data yourself as scatter plots, and then showing merged bars to the audience if the relationships to be featured are clear in merged bars.

Believe it or not, we're *still* not quite done with scatter plots (!) because there's a second, entirely different type of scatter plot that I haven't even mentioned yet. Allow me to introduce...

"ITEM-COMPARISON" SCATTER PLOTS

Have a look at the scatter plot below, which shows an organization's current sales prospects based on the probability that they'll close each prospect as a customer, along with each prospect's estimated revenue potential:

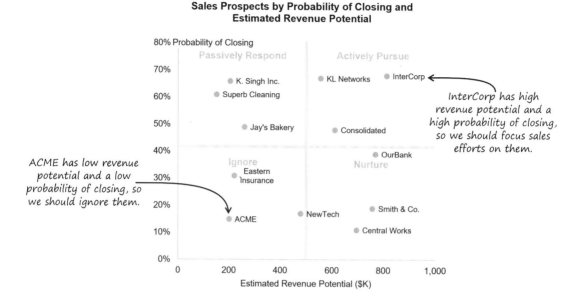

An "item-comparison" scatter plot

Sales Prospects by Probability of Closing and Estimated Revenue Potential

InterCorp has high revenue potential and a high probability of closing, so we should focus sales efforts on them.

ACME has low revenue potential and a low probability of closing, so we should ignore them.

This chart is pretty useful because it shows which sales prospects the organization should focus on and which ones they should ignore.

Although the scatter plot above *looks* like the correlation scatter plots that we've seen so far, its purpose is fundamentally different. The purpose of this scatter plot *isn't* to show how the "Probability of Closing" variable is related to the "Estimated Revenue Potential" variable. Sure, that relationship *can* be seen as a pattern of dots, but that's not what this chart is *for*. The purpose of this chart is to show how a set of items (i.e., Sales Prospects) *compare with one another*. For example, a key takeaway from this chart might be that InterCorp is a much better sales prospect than ACME. That's why I call this second type of scatter plot an "item-comparison" scatter plot, not a "correlation" scatter plot.

This fundamental difference in purpose makes the guidelines for designing item-comparison scatter plots quite different than those for designing correlation scatter plots. For example, in an item-comparison scatter plot…

Most or all the dots must be labeled.

Because item-comparison scatter plots are for comparing *individual items* with one another, it's necessary to label most or all the dots individually so that the audience knows, for example, which dot represents which sales prospect. In fact, item-comparison scatter plots are basically *useless* if the dots aren't labeled. **In a correlation scatter plot, however, it's rarely useful or necessary to label all the dots.**

Quadrants are useful.

Item-comparison scatter plots almost always benefit from being divided into *regions* (e.g., quadrants) with helpful labels for each region. For example, the "Sales Prospects" scatter plot above is divided into useful regions labeled "Actively Pursue," "Nurture," "Passively Respond," and "Ignore." Indeed, item-comparison scatter plots are so often divided into a two-region by two-region grid that many people call them "two-by-two matrices." **In a correlation scatter plot, however, dividing the chart area into regions generally isn't helpful.**

Trendlines are unhelpful or confusing.

As we saw earlier, adding trendlines or other relationship summarization features can be quite useful in *correlation* scatter plots. In *item-comparison* scatter plots, however, the relationship between the two variables is generally irrelevant, so **adding trendlines or other relationship summarization features is unhelpful in item-comparison scatter plots, and is usually confusing:**

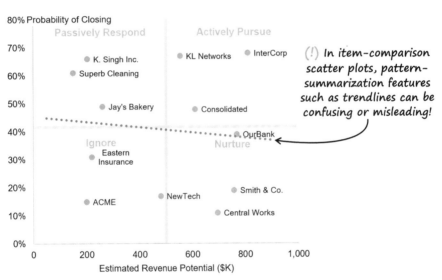

Now that you know how to recognize item-comparison scatter plots, you'll probably see them all over the place, and there's a good chance that you'll find yourself needing to create them yourself. Because the guidelines for designing item-comparison scatter plots are quite different than those for designing correlation scatter plots, it's essential to:

- Understand that there are *two* types of scatter plots, not one, as many chart creators assume.

- Be able to recognize whether you're creating a "correlation" scatter plot or an "item-comparison" scatter plot so that you can apply the appropriate set of design guidelines for the type of scatter plot that you're creating.

What, exactly, are the guidelines for designing item-comparison scatter plots? Here you go...

CHEAT SHEET:
FORMATTING "ITEM-COMPARISON" SCATTER PLOTS

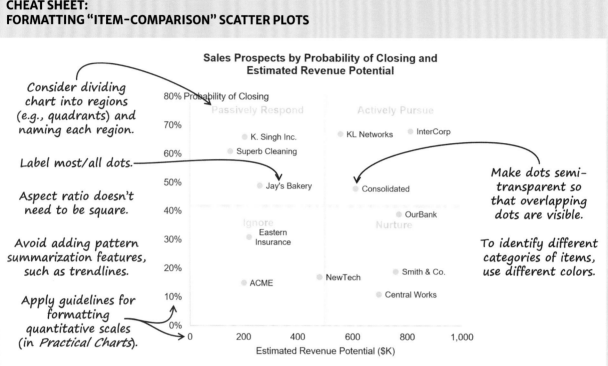

Key takeaways: Item-comparison scatter plots

- The term "scatter plot" is used to refer to two quite different chart types: correlation scatter plots and item-comparison scatter plots.
- The purposes and design guidelines for item-comparison scatter plots are quite different from those for correlation scatter plots.

The data in an item-comparison scatter plot can generally also be shown as...

Merged bar charts (for item comparison)

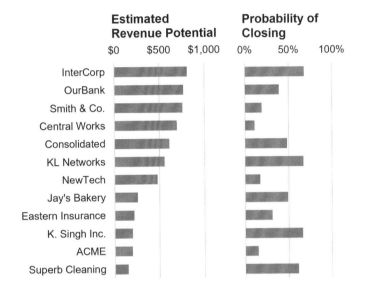

As you can see, a merged bar chart can show many of the same insights as an item-comparison scatter plot and, as we saw earlier, audiences generally find merged bar charts easier to understand than scatter plots.

> Why use item–comparison scatter plots, then? Why not always use merged bars to compare items?

There are two main reasons why I generally use scatter plots rather than merged bars for item comparison:

- Item-comparison scatter plots make it a little quicker to spot, for example, the best sales prospects (i.e., the dots in the upper right). You *can* see this kind of thing in a merged bar chart (just look for sales prospects with two long bars), but it's quicker in an item-comparison scatter plot.

- Although they're a little more complex than merged bar charts, item-comparison scatter plots are easier to understand than *correlation* scatter plots because item-comparison scatter plots don't require the audience to understand the concept of correlation, or how to interpret different dot patterns. The audience just needs to understand that, for example, dots in the upper-right region are good sales prospects. This is even easier to understand if the chart is divided into labeled regions (e.g., "Actively Pursue," "Ignore," etc.) since the region labels act as "duh insights."

How items compare with one another generally isn't set in stone and can change over time, and you might find yourself needing to show those changes to an audience, so let's briefly talk about…

Showing item comparisons changing over time

To show how items compared with one another over time, you can add "trails" to the dots in an item-comparison scatter plot to show how they "moved" over time:

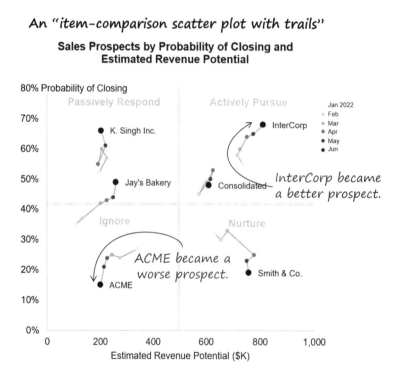

You might have noticed that item-comparison scatter plots with trails are also *connected scatter plots*, like the ones that I recommended against using earlier, but I'm recommending them in this case. What gives? The short answer is that I don't think that connecting the dots in an *item-comparison* scatter plot causes the same perceptual challenges as connecting dots in a *correlation* scatter plot. Having said that, if there are many time periods and/or the trails are very convoluted, this chart type can get messy, as well. To learn more about when I think connected scatter plots are and aren't a good idea, visit practicalreporting.com/pc-resources, and click "About connected scatter plots."

Key takeaway: Showing item comparisons changing over time

- To show how a set of items compare with one another over time, consider using an item-comparison scatter plot with trails.

Alright, now that you know about both types of scatter plots, we finally have everything we need for the…

DECISION TREE:
CHOOSING A CHART TYPE TO SHOW CORRELATION OR ITEM COMPARISON

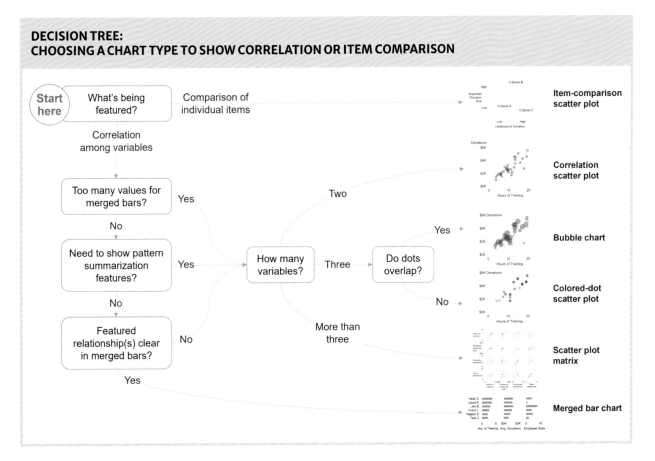

Now, I should mention that there's actually a *third* type of scatter plot, which I call a "distribution scatter plot," whose main purpose is to show how a set of items is distributed along two variables. Distribution scatter plots require a considerable amount of expertise to read, however, so they generally aren't used for everyday charts. The other distribution chart types that we saw in the previous chapter (strip plots, histograms, etc.) usually do the trick when showing distributions in everyday reports and presentations.

Before we leave correlation charts behind, I want to briefly mention…

INSET CHARTS (IN CORRELATION CHARTS)

What if there are values in your correlation data that are far larger than the other values (i.e., the data contains outliers)? As we saw in *Practical Charts*, inset charts can be used to handle outliers in most chart types, including correlation charts:

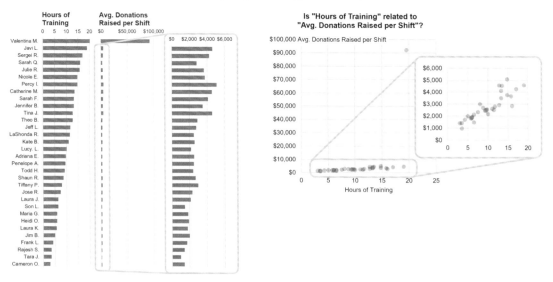

Use inset charts to handle outliers in correlation charts
(or virtually any other type of chart).

That's it for correlation and item-comparison charts, the final family of chart types that we'll see in this book. So…

Conclusion

What now?

With the 30 chart types that we saw in *Practical Charts* and the 20 or so in this book, you now have a "vocabulary" of about 50 chart types (not including the dozen or so that I don't recommend for everyday charts). If you weren't using the 20 "advanced" chart types in this book before, perhaps you might start using them in your work, now that you've seen how useful they can be.

As I mentioned at the beginning of this book, "advanced" is, of course, a relative term. There are plenty of other advanced chart types that we didn't cover, but, in my experience, you'll probably only need those if you work in a specialized domain such as genomics, advanced mathematics, or mineral exploration.

As usual, there's always more to learn. Where should you go next? A few suggestions:

More specialized chart types

If you *do* work in a specialized domain such as genomics or mineral exploration, you might need to use specialized chart types that we didn't cover. If that's the case, I hope that you'll be able to extrapolate from the examples and guidelines in this book and in *Practical Charts* to help you design those specialized chart types effectively.

If your work *doesn't* require you to go beyond the 50 chart types in these books, you might still keep an eye out for interesting new chart types anyway. I always learn something from interpreting a chart type that I haven't seen before, even if I never end up using that chart type in my own work.

Information dashboards

If your work requires you to create arrangements of related charts on a single display (i.e., dashboards), that entails a whole other set of challenges. For recommended courses and books on dashboard design, please visit practicalreporting.com/pc-resources and click "Recommended books and courses."

If it's out by the time you read this, you might also consider reading my next book, *Practical Dashboards*, which is expected to be published in 2024.

Charts for analysis

As I mentioned in the introductory chapters of *Practical Charts*, that book and this one only discuss charts for communicating data to other people. As you probably know, charts can also be a very powerful way to *explore data and discover new insights on your own* by making charts that no one will see but you. As you can probably imagine, the guidelines for creating charts for yourself can be quite different than those for creating charts for communicating data to other people.

For recommended books and courses on using charts for data analysis, visit practicalreporting. com/pc-resources and click "Recommended books and courses." I'm also planning to write a book about using charts for analysis, but the publication date for that book hasn't been set as I write this in 2023.

Data art, infographics, data journalism pieces, etc.

As you know, *Practical Charts* and this book only discuss "everyday" charts for reports and presentations, that is, charts where the goal is to communicate specific insights or answers as clearly and quickly as possible. That's definitely not the case for *all* data visualizations, though. There are many situations in which the point of a visualization is to maximize aesthetic or emotional appeal, or to demonstrate original, creative ways to visualize data. For recommended books and courses on creating these and other types of visualizations, please visit practicalreporting.com/pc-resources and click "Recommended books and courses."

If you decide to explore these or any other areas, I wish you the happiest of trails.

Bonne chance, mon ami,

Nick

P.S.: If you found these books to be valuable, I'd be deliriously grateful if you were to post a short review of *Practical Charts* on Amazon, other major book-selling or book review sites, a personal blog, and/or social media. Amazon reviews in particular can make a big difference in helping others to discover these books. If you decide to post a review of *Practical Charts*, let me know on Twitter (@nickdesb) or LinkedIn (search for "Nick Desbarats"). Even if you don't post a review, feel free to connect with me on those platforms or sign up for my email list at www.practicalreporting.com to stay in touch.

Index